Demandir ....ocracy:
The Case for a Scottish Media

Christopher Silver

WP
BOOKS

Published by Word Power Books 2015
43–45 West Nicolson Street
Edinburgh EH8 9DB
www.word-power.co.uk

Printed and bound by Bell & Bain, Scotland.
Front cover illustration copyright © Andrew Redmond Barr
Designed by Leela Sooben

British Library Cataloguing in Publication Data.
A catalogue record for this book is available from the British Library.
ISBN 978-0-9927392-8-7

Author's Note

At the age of 17 I was at school and I was bored. So I walked down to the offices of a local newspaper and asked for a job. A few weeks later I became a trainee reporter on one of the shortest lived and most disastrously managed local newspapers to have ever made it off a printing press. The *Shetland Weekly* was my first foray into journalism. I was soon to witness walkouts, redundancies, a whole range of bad behaviour and the ultimate liquidation of the company within a year. It was, perhaps, a fitting introduction to the world of Scottish journalism. Not least because I personally succeeded in alienating large sections of the paper's fledgling readership. Remarkably, I was not put off. The experience of collapse is fascinating and perhaps this is why colleagues from that time still remember the whole sorry episode with a remarkable degree of fondness. For my part, despite heading out into a field in which any form of remuneration was becoming increasingly scarce, I've continued to write and produce media in various forms ever since. The secret to what makes the recent crisis of the Scottish media so compelling may lie therein – for many such work is more of a compulsion, an addiction even, than a career choice. No member of the small band still working in the Scottish media could be daft enough to mistake it for the latter.

The intermittent risk of poverty that goes along with writing anything of any value is of course one of the most daunting realities any writer has to face. In my case I was exceptionally fortunate to be able to crowdfund the research phase of this book in February 2015. As a result, in a very direct sense, this book only exists due to the generosity of the 110 contributors who allowed me to commit serious amounts of time to it. The remarkable contributions of Steven Keith, Elaine Fraser and Heather Leith should be highlighted in their own right. If this book can begin a nation-wide conversation about our media I am confident such investment will prove fruitful and farsighted.

My purpose in writing this book was to synthesise the ideas and experiences shared with me by numerous journalists, writers and academics who were kind enough to donate their time to the conversations that underpin it. Wherever possible, I have quoted their thoughts at length and feel confident that this work is rooted in a range of expertise far greater than my own. Scotland's headlong journey towards a future very different from its current state is still ongoing. This fact, above all else, demanded that this work of map-making involve as much intelligent reflection as I could gather. Talking to individuals each with decades of experience seemed like the best route to achieve this.

Particular gratitude goes out to Elaine and Tarlochan – the stalwarts behind Word Power Books. In an exceptionally difficult year, they stuck with this project and were prepared to put up with my own deadline busting habits, as the scope of this book varied over the course of the year. In their willingness to support new Scottish voices and radical politics, Word Power Books play a valuable role in contemporary Scotland's intellectual and imaginative life. A fitting tribute to this is to take their advice and boycott exploitative giants like Amazon and buy from their website instead.

I am also grateful for the support of the following colleagues and friends for their freely offered help, support and advice: Alison Balharry, David Greig, Mairi McFadyen, Andrew Redmond Barr, Stephen Greenhorn, Sarah Beattie Smith, Andy Summers, Stuart Campbell, Daniel Chaplin, Lucy Harwood, Michael Gray, Angela Haggerty, Al McMaster, Mike Small, Jack Foster, Carolyn Scott, James Devoy, Tina Sieber, Robin McAlpine, Dominic Hinde, Maurice Smith, and Peter Geoghegan.

Introduction

On the 22 November 2014 I looked out across a sea of saltires, yellow foam fingers and tiny smartphone screens that filled the vast expanse of Glasgow's SSE Hydro Arena. The Scottish National Party (SNP) and its newly bolstered membership was in town: tens of thousands had joined in the weeks and months following the bitter disappointment of 19 September. The phenomenal growth of the SNP, unprecedented in modern politics, had stunned many commentators who had assumed that a No vote would put an abrupt halt to its steady insurgency since 2007. The event was a slickly produced political spectacle – from the massive LED screen at the back of the stage, adorned with hundreds of selfies sent in from individual members – to the gold glitter cannons that brought the event to a close. With a sell-out audience of 12,000, the event was live streamed, participants were encouraged to tweet photos and get a hashtag trending, there were bands and a roving camera crew. As speaker after speaker pointed out, such a gathering had never before been seen in douce old Scotland. If you'd replaced the saltires with the stars and stripes this could have been a party convention in the United States: it had the scale, the brashness and the production values. Members of the press in attendance seemed a bit taken aback by the whole thing. *BuzzFeed*'s Jamie Ross described it as 'the strangest political event in Scotland since Robert the Bruce felt it was appropriate to take leadership advice from a spider.'[1] Here was a political party, whose *raison d'etre* had slipped from its grasp just two months earlier, joyously re-incarnating itself in sight of the masses.

Who was this event for? On one level it was just a good old-fashioned rally, but it was also, in every sense of the word a *media* event. It marked the culmination of a month-long tour by Nicola Sturgeon and the remarkable fact that the SNP could now claim to be Scotland's only mass membership party. At one point, the latest, ever increasing tally of new recruits flashed up on the screen: 90,263. With more than one in sixty Scots now within its ranks and as the third largest party by membership in the UK, it now requires its own vehicle to speak to this vast new audience and to show off its youthful new media credentials. But the Hydro wasn't just a display of the organisation's massive new proportions, it was also a demonstration of its ability to bypass traditional media channels. In doing so, on such a scale, it was sending a message to Scotland's media establishment: we didn't need your support anyway.

The event also answered a hitherto unasked question: how do you follow Alex Salmond at an SNP gig? The answer, as I still recall with some disbelief, was celtic-rock band the Red Hot Chilli Pipers, playing 'Don't Stop Believing.' Salmond, having formally resigned as First Minister three days earlier, was now only a support act. Taking to the vast stage he noted, 'In the referendum campaign there were 33 newspaper titles in this country. One of them was in favour of independence, two of them were neutral and 30 were against,' before piling novelty upon novelty with news that a brand new newspaper, the *National*, would be launched the following Monday. Salmond endorsed the new product and encouraged supporters to, 'make sure that this pro-independence daily is a great success and let's redress the balance of the old with a new title in Scotland.' At one point, compere John Nicolson (who has since been elected MP for East Dunbartonshire and is now the Party's Westminster spokesperson for Culture, Media and Sport) announced, 'Now Nicola was telling me backstage … that she now has more Twitter followers than the *Scotsman* has readers. So how about we get the Hydro trending on Twitter?' If this was the referendum Yes vs No battle being recast as New vs Old media, it was remarkably hard to tell who was the underdog and who stood triumphantly ensconced. In a pointed remark Salmond expressed a clear desire to shake up Scottish broadcasting too, '…and thinking about our position in the world, how we see the world, and how the world sees Scotland,' he mused, 'isn't it vitally important that we have a true public service broadcaster in this nation?' Richard Walker, editor of the *Sunday Herald*, and the soon to be *National*, would later tell the crowd, 'I went to a newsagent this morning and there were … more than 20 newspapers on sale in Scotland, how many of them supported independence or support independence? You know the answer to that, the answer is: none.' To rapturous applause he added, 'On Monday there will be *one*.'

Announcing the launch of a national daily newspaper at a party rally led to inevitable criticisms of the *National*, which, whatever its flaws, still hits the newsstands on a daily basis. In contrast, in 2005 an attempt at a weekly pro-independence title, the *Scottish Standard*, folded after only seven weeks.[2] For some the *National's* content just doesn't cut it and it's not yet clear how secure the new title actually is in a notoriously cannibalistic industry. Walker's deal with owners Newsquest was bound to lead to a visibly precarious product – based, as it was, on an insistence that the paper had to prove its viability in a weekly trial before a serious financial commitment was made.

Standing in the midst of Scotland's brave new world of stadium politics I couldn't help but wonder where such euphoria would go. For all the awkward segues and the vast amounts of corporate hype, the Hydro succeeded in underlining (even to the most cynical punter) that Scotland was not the place it had once been. The Hydro was a landmark, a staging post on the road towards the SNP's unprecedented triumph in the May 2015 general election.

Never before had a party in Scotland hosted such an audacious event. This was mass political participation in an age that we are told is defined by a crisis of apathy. Such momentum was at least partly borne upon a sense of injustice, not least that inflicted by what was perceived as a client, pro-union, media. These were people who had been told by a succession of lurid headlines that to vote Yes would mean, amongst other things: betraying those slain in former conflicts, setting back progress on a cure for cancer, border posts, financial armageddon and a new 'great depression.' Pensions, families, even marriages, were all at risk. This media onslaught was as shrill as it was broad based. An unprecedented and overwhelmingly reactionary posture was adopted across the ideological spectrum represented in the British press. Will Hutton, writing in the *Guardian* just days before polls opened, suggested Scottish independence represented 'the death of the liberal enlightenment before the atavistic forces of nationalism and ethnicity – a dark omen for the 21st century.'[3] With the majority of newspapers favouring negative stories about the referendum a narrative was presented that was bound to favour the pro-UK campaign. For many, the push for continued union, or 'Project Fear' as it called itself, was a blatant stitch up that was only made possible by the complicity of media organisations and the three big UK parties. Yet neither the anguish provoked by such unfettered media hysteria, nor the gut reaction to switch-off from it, offers a way to move beyond this rupture.

Today, there remains an inescapable anomaly in Scottish public life. The rapid growth of a political party and a whole new movement striving towards the aim of independence has not met with the support of a single editor, with the exception of Walker. No other newspaper was prepared to contemplate backing independence, not even as a cynical means to boost ailing circulation. Yet, whether we like it or not, Scotland is now a country in which the First Minister has vastly more Twitter followers than several national newspapers have readers. In August 2015 Sturgeon would reflect on how significant social media has been in her own career stating, 'The ability to communicate so directly and so quickly with so many people is hugely valuable … it allows me, if I so choose, to bypass or, on occasion, challenge traditional media.'[4] A political party set against the established order still courts press favour to an extent, but it does so with a new media swagger that suggests it is almost passé.

The SNP's success is itself part of a wider process in Scottish politics that has been underway for decades. The great irony, as we shall see, is that while the media's coverage of the referendum failed to grasp the broad character of Yes as a social movement, its coverage solidified a post-referendum desire for continued agency that ended up expressing itself in the gathering of mammoth levels of support for the SNP (and to a lesser extent the Scottish Greens and Scottish Socialists). But the movement-based approach of Yes did not play well with the press or broadcasters, sitting as it did largely beyond the realm of professional contacts, other journalists and spin-doctors. In Scotland the referendum gathered a rapid level of grassroots momentum – on the streets, in pubs and community halls – it was marked out by its distinctly non-establishment character. As this momentum channelled itself into Sturgeon's freshly rebooted SNP, its scope, its scale and its arguments became impossible to ignore between September 2014 and May 2015.

The SNP's growth has been fuelled by a reluctance in wider Scottish society to understand and engage with what the Party actually represents. As of July 2015 membership stands at 110,000, it won a 50% share of the vote in the 2015 general election. It has fundamentally redrawn the electoral map of Scotland and totally altered the dynamics of UK politics. But no single party can represent an entire nation. To think it can do so reduces that nation to the status of a single constituency, rather than a place of multitudes. The risk is not some hysterical vision of a one party state. Rather, it is to repeat the mistakes of Scotland's recent political past: to live in a country that is run by special interests, professional elites, institutions and a party that comes to confuse its *mandate* for a divine right to rule. In displaying loyalty to one political faction, a narrowness of focus of which both the political and media establishment have often been guilty, goes some of the way to explaining why Scotland is often referred to as a tribal country. It is for this reason that, as the strange case of the Hydro attests, partisan media is no kind of substitute for a modern multi-channel media. Amidst the still raw confusion and emotion, the media fallout from the referendum does clearly demonstrate that no amount of negative coverage from above can stem the tide of a popular movement. To insist, as many bastions of unionism still do, that these people are the 'other', is only to make them stronger, louder and that bit more gallus. The Hydro was brought into being by Scotland's media. A media that many felt had become a contender in a debate in which passions ran high, but in which violence was entirely absent and bad behaviour overwhelmingly restricted to the darker recesses of social media. A certain blindness in Scotland's media has in effect hardened and compressed a multiform social movement into an immensely powerful political machine. On some news days it may think the opposite, but the broader picture is clear: this creation cannot go back into its box.

***

In modern societies, media – from the earliest pamphlets, broadsides and newsheets to today's global mediascape – are a fundamental part of how contemporary society sustains itself. The set of institutions, practices, products and markets that we call 'the media' is often flawed. Certainly, it is as capable of perpetrating private evils as it is at upholding public good. Yet in a complex society like our own, it is the only means that we have to talk to and understand one another. Since the great transformations that have shaped modernity took place: from rural to urban, from commu-

INTRODUCTION   9

nity to body politic and from locality to nation, we have required media technologies to allow communication, culture, debate and dialogue to take place *en masse*. While this process has often served to concentrate power and smother dissent, as we will see, the field is far more contested than it first appears.

The problems facing Scotland's media are so pervasive and manifest on so many different fronts it can be hard to characterise in simple terms. Perhaps we might call it a state of inertia. Or, we might simply reflect that everyday, brilliant, complex and fascinating stories unfold in Scotland and that if we do not start to address our media deficit, we risk losing our ability to tell them altogether. This book will seek to take a broader view as we contemplate stepping out from the old and into a new kind of media space with confidence. It will consider how we might map this new territory. This book offers starting points, it positions some key questions in a manner that is clear and accessible, but the answers are so closely related to democracy itself that they can only be found through a wider dialogue.

For the moment it is enough to assert that, based on widely understood concepts about what 'the media' does, a nation without one must be a nation lacking a great deal. In the Scottish context, we have tended to think of these problems in terms of single solutions. Often these ideas are smart, legitimate and deeply necessary, but there is no neat solution to a problem so complex. In global terms, media, like Scotland itself, are witnessing a sustained period of flux. On both fronts it is worth starting from the premise that in order to work out the coordinates of future travel, we need to be sharp when recollecting where we have been.

In the following essays, I do not claim to offer a comprehensive history of the Scottish media – much has been omitted that might have found its way into a longer study. Think of this book instead as a provocation: my own narration about a set of institutions that are among the strangest, the most distinct and indeed the most neglected in this country's history. We'll look at some of the most compelling cases of triumph and ruin in Scotland's print and broadcast media, while also considering the cultural aspects of the debate and the emergence of alternative media in recent years.

The backdrop to which this book has been written could scarcely have been more febrile. It has been completed in the wake of a far closer referendum on independence than anyone predicted, and in that event's unexpected epilogue – a general election result that saw pundits desperately reaching for new metaphors as terms like 'seismic' and 'tsunami' lost their meaning through overuse. However, the impetus for this work goes back beyond the referendum. It has its roots in a strong personal desire to explore the problems that Scotland's media faces in more depth and with more consideration than they have hitherto been afforded.

In trying to fathom the causes behind such a glaring anomaly: that a country with a national politics should not have a national media, I was moved to tell a story about professional storytellers, to start a public conversation about the organisations that we trust with that task. Above all, I have sought to question a status quo that offers only a semblance of stability and in which few feel well served. The imperative is democratic in the broadest sense. It is explicitly not a matter of partisan politics – whatever faction might or might not gain from a media revival in Scotland is far from clear – but it is self-evident that the polity as a whole would be greatly enriched.

Scotland lacks the media structures required of a modern nation. Even in comparison to other semi-autonomous regions its media remains overwhelmingly metropolitan. But this chronic marginality also offers us a space to innovate. If we demand the right to start all over again in Scotland, to build a new national media that expresses the best of Scottish traditions, it could offer a model for rebooting a trade so often compromised by the complexities of the information age. There is no 'answer' to the lack of something other than the will to imagine, to create, and to build something new.

1

A Democratic Deficit

The referendum was a perfect storm that ripped an already rickety Scottish media from its moorings. Meanwhile, democracy was the watchword of the campaign itself. It was used to rally and console, to validate a momentous phase in Scottish politics. In the UK, the press are not governed by democratic structures or constitutional obligations: newspaper ownership is largely seen as an issue best left to the market. In Scotland's case, this means that with the exception of the secretive DC Thomson stable, no national newspaper title is currently owned in Scotland. For broadcasters, an insistence on presenting the referendum as a *de-facto* party political contest often resulted in dull, repetitive and inherently confrontational coverage. What was sorely lacking in the Scottish media landscape was plurality. Richard Walker's team at the *Sunday Herald* would seek to redress this, with an acute awareness that journalism in Scotland had a duty to offer choice in terms of editorial opinion. Though the move to become explicitly pro-independence was decried by many, as *Sunday Herald* columnist Ian Bell explains, Walker's motive was not nationalism, but fairness, 'He thought the status quo simply wasn't fair, either to Yes supporters or the wider public. He was right.' Bell's comment is prescient for the following discussion and the argument that I want to put forward. The dominance of one position in any sphere of democratic life, whether in the press corps or in a parliament chamber, can never be healthy.

This is about much more than grudge or the bad treatment of any single position. It is, quite simply, a question of democracy.

Why Media Matters

The word media in itself is a difficult starting point. Grammatically it's the plural of medium, but in modern usage the term refers to the content and structure of the medium too. In our global society, this small word refers to a vast array of organisations, professions, behaviours, products, services and marketplaces. As society has developed and become more complex and interconnected, the range, variety and aims of media have exploded. As if that wasn't confusing enough, in the information age everything is refracted, from the vast and cosmic to the intimate and personal, through some form of media lens. But this isn't just a passive process: as individuals we act, we transmit, we publish, we share, we broadcast. Manuel Castells calls this 'mass self-communication,' a useful term for the vast changes that have occurred through the emergence of digital technology in recent decades.[5] Increasingly, people behave like tiny media organisations and often carry out, for free, functions that were once only accessible to a select few: commenting, reporting, discussing and witnessing.

All too often, this mass proliferation of media jams our ability to comprehend what is actually going on. It becomes mere noise. But somewhere in between the adventures of a particularly intrepid kitten and the inner workings of the Hadron Collider, we receive a residual summary of what is actually happening elsewhere. We call this news. Some of us still like it a day old in all its black and white printed certainty. Defining what that approximate impression (papery or otherwise) consists of, is a massively important task. We glorify it, we demonise it, because as a profoundly significant act it can demonstrate both the most noble and the most despicable forms of human behaviour. Some hack dead people's phones for gossip, others sacrifice their lives in order to help us understand the awfulness of human suffering that is happening elsewhere, now. Both get lumped together within a trade that we call journalism.

Today journalism and the industries that support it are staring into the abyss. The trade of deciding what is current has become lost in a throng of hawkers competing for our attention in the global media village. Vast and shiny new miracle workers (like Google) are taking its livelihood, while rarely attempting to adopt its lofty aims and weighty responsibilities. The internet giants are becoming an ever more dominant part of the media mix, but they don't dispatch teams in flak jackets to cover conflict zones, or sift through the tedium of party conferences and international summits for a clear story. Overwhelmingly those tasks still fall to state funded broad- casters and old media corporations. Meanwhile, advertisers only care who serves their product to the biggest audience and as a result vehicles for journalism are increasingly called upon to innovate. They're asked to do so as PR experts and spin-doctors exert ever more pressure on a smaller and smaller group of professional news gatherers. Increasingly, it is the former group: those who are paid to turn a private agenda into a matter of public interest, that define what is delivered to us as news. Faced with a constant barrage of pre-packaged stories, the working lives of journalists are increas- ingly spent in centralised offices: factory farms in which only the exceptionally lucky or talented are allowed to roam in the real world. Of course, there is no 'golden age' to hark back to here. Journalism has long been seen as a grubby, boozy, malicious trade, while elites and vested interests have been attempting to coerce it for centuries. Yet in the formative years of our 'information society' developing a greater awareness of how news is framed and selected has become a matter of paramount importance. We must assert the right to greater understanding or risk the erosion of personal and collective freedoms. This, essentially, is the outline of coming struggles every-where: to make information more accessible and to liberate the interpretation of it from the straightjacket of private, commercial funding models that are crumbling all around us.

This global picture brings us to the specific shape of the issues facing Scotland. Overall, its media landscape looks increasingly bleak. As once proud titles like the *Scotsman* are becoming ever more squeezed and even start-ups like the *National* are expected to run on a shoestring, the information that gets passed down to us becomes inevitably more biased and less likely to be tested against objective criteria. There are a host of new media initiatives chal-lenging this, most of which are run on minuscule resources and are largely funded through donations. The biggest abnormality about post-devolution Scotland is that just as the Scottish Parliament was signalling a genuine sense of democratic renewal, one of the most vital aspects in a democracy – a vigorous, multi-channel media – would see its prestige rapidly erode. The story of BBC Radio Scotland is a case in point. Award winning and widely respected for its current affairs output in the 1990s, its now neglected state moved Professor Tom Devine to reflect in 2012 on 'the sad decline of a once influential organisation.'[6]

While a whole new arena for representation was unveiling itself at Holyrood, managerialism and commercial decline would savage the resources available to both major newspaper titles and current affairs programmes like *Good Morning Scotland*. How, we might ask, could a media under such strain perform its own representative task? Or did the new Scotland heralded by devo-lution fall short of the vibrant young democracy that was hoped for? Certainly the scandals of various sizes that enveloped the new Scottish Parliament did not create the impression that the early days of a better nation had arrived. As Gerry Hassan argues, the reconvening of the parliament led to a narrowing of public life as the chamber itself became the focal point for public debate:

... the absence of public forums, other than the Scottish Parliament and specialist platforms, made public debate and conversations remarkably narrow and elitist, with the public reduced to inactive bystanders and the state of the national mood unknown (beyond opinion polls having to be second-guessed).[7]

Given the somewhat lacklustre approach of the Scottish establishment to opening up politics in Scotland beyond the confines of Holyrood, it is perhaps unsurprising that the surge in digital media opened up a vital new space for discussion about the nation's politics. The diversity available offers an obvious point of comparison with the Scottish press. Nowhere was the post-devolution development of a narrow and elitist view of Scottish public life more apparent than in the reluctance of Scottish newspapers to reconsider the question of independence. Back in 2004 journalist Murray Ritchie noted:

Most Scottish newspapers are downright hostile to independence and those which are not are mainly indifferent. This is an auld sang, and an affront to democracy and free expression. Indeed it is more than that because it amounts to a conspiratorial denial of the existence of a political ambition which is attractive - sometimes obsessively so - to a significant section of the electorate.[8]

It was against this problematic backdrop that the question of Scottish independence was put to the people of Scotland in an unprecedented two year campaign. As that debate began to gather momentum it was mirrored by a sense of disconnect as every daily newspaper indulged in reactionary and partisan headlines about the impact of a Yes vote. The media was found to be wanting in Scotland, not because of the performance of any individual journalist, but because, in a number of crucial ways, the set of institutions that we refer to as the Scottish media has little structural form, often it exists in name only. In terms of media products that seek to be 'national' in their output, behind the scenes, there is a notable lack of structural control in Scotland. This, above all else, is why we must make a compelling case for a new Scottish media.

Was There a Scottish Media?

In starting from the premise that there is not a Scottish media, there are a few basic points that need to be made clear before going any further. Firstly, it is not to suggest that Scotland does not have the ability to sustain a national media. The often thriving media ecologies of neighbouring small countries with similar populations show that a re-structured and emboldened Scottish media could be viable. Secondly, it is not to claim that the lack of a national media for Scotland is due to the laziness or incompetence of media professionals in Scotland – far from it, there is a centuries old tradition of exporting Scottish talent – the point is to ask why it often seems so keen to leave. Thirdly, as will be discussed in Chapter 5, there was a historic window when Scotland did have a distinct print-based media culture of its own, the significance of which cannot be underestimated. Finally, there are numerous examples of Scotland producing indigenous news, current affairs and cultural content that is second to none. That such instances are not the norm is a massive indictment of the status quo that these pages seek to challenge. Whatever else might be contentious about the state of Scotland's media there is a wealth of evidence that when Scottish producers, editors, journalists, writers, or directors are afforded proper time and resources, they are as capable as anyone else of creating quality, occasionally groundbreaking, work.

Nonetheless, the *media in Scotland,* such as it is, is in crisis. This crisis is taking place on a number of levels and the symptoms are manifold. They include systemic declines in newspaper staff numbers and circulation, a crisis of morale and legitimacy at BBC Scotland and acutely damaging managerial cultures intent on doing more with less. Post-referendum, there is a real risk of the formation of 'old' and 'new' media echo chambers. While the technological challenges facing media institutions really are of a global nature, there are certain local conditions in Scotland that continue to stifle progress too. For some, the countless changes to the way we consume media are a cause for optimism, others can only see (barring some as yet unknowable innovations that might make journalism commercially viable again) a bleak picture. There is not space here to look into the many possible futures for a global mediascape that is still very much in flux. What we can do is consider some of the implications the media's deficient state had on the most significant democratic event in Scottish history.

Reporting Risk

In 2014 I interviewed veteran Scottish politician Jim Sillars at his Edinburgh home. Perhaps unsurprisingly, the former Depute Leader of the SNP expressed dismay at coverage of the referendum. While noting that STV's coverage had been 'much fairer', he told me, 'I think the BBC is an absolute disgrace. I think the *Scotsman* is a disgrace and I don't think the other newspapers rank much better...' Though characteristically uncompromising, Sillars was expressing a view that was widely held by many Yes campaigners. 'I don't mind a newspaper being opposed to independence,' he added, ' ... there's a difference between having an editorial line, which promotes one particular position, but it should be incumbent on any media that tries to serve the whole community to at least balance, to some extent, its coverage instead of giving over totally to negativity.'

For the avoidance of doubt, in the UK at least, the press is not under any statutory duty to offer balance. The Independent Press Standards Organisation (IPSO) states clearly within its Editors' Code of Practice that newspapers, 'whilst free to be partisan, must distinguish clearly between comment, conjecture and fact.'[9] Yet, as groups such as Hacked Off and the Media Standards Trust have pointed out, IPSO lacks explicit power to compel the press to print corrections or implement fines, falling well short of standards in other European countries, and for that matter the recommendations of the Leveson Inquiry that led to its creation.[10] Furthermore, the code does not impinge on an editor's ability to place an inflammatory or provocative headline above more nuanced copy, something that became common practice during the referendum campaign. The importance of headlines is particularly significant online, where studies have found that only a fraction of visitors scroll down to read a full article.[11] But the frustration that Sillars expressed, founded on a deep suspicion of unscrupulous behaviour in much of the press, touches on an issue that is not unique to Scotland, even if the spotlight of the referendum ended up exposing how acute the problem had become.

Citing an announcement on 30 May 2014 by Ivan Menzies, CEO of drinks giant Diageo, which controls 40% of Scottish whisky production, Sillars railed against the perceived failure of journalists to scrutinise the claims of big business in more detail:

> If someone comes up with a stupid statement about Scotland ... Diageo ... are telling us that if we're independent they'll have a problem selling *whisky* worldwide. This is an absolute utter nonsense. So why, when their PR bumf comes in, why does the reporter not phone Diageo and say, "we've got a couple of questions to ask you...where

is the problem in selling whisky if Scotland is independent? Is something happening in that distillery? What is
happening?" They should lay bare that kind of nonsense,
but they don't, they report it as if it's one of the gospel
truths.

The *Guardian* and *The Times* ran the announcement without putting
questions to Diageo, or offering an alternative view.[12] [13] On 31 May
2014 the *Herald* ran the story alongside warnings on independence
from other business leaders, including the CEOs of B&Q and BAE
systems, though it did print a response to these remarks from pro-
independence group Business for Scotland.[14]

The question that follows on from the point raised by Sillars, is
why such announcements, particularly from large corporations,
often seem to be taken at face value by journalists? Nick Robinson's question to Alex Salmond on 11 September became notorious
for a claim in the resultant package that the First Minister 'didn't
answer' warnings from the corporate sector on independence.
However, the outrage provoked by the omission of Salmond's
response missed a far bigger issue about the nature of how the
question was framed. Robinson asked the First Minister, 'Why
should a Scottish voter believe you, a politician, against men
who are responsible for billions of pounds of profits?' a question loaded with a familiar mentality in which journalists are
often inclined to take an uncritical view of statements from business leaders, while politicians are viewed as suspect. The logical
counter-question, 'why should a voter believe men who are
responsible for billions of pounds of profits?' was rarely, if ever,
posed to the business community. A failure to interrogate such
statements and a tendency to refer to them as objective sources
was inherently, if not explicitly, likely to favour a No campaign
that was seeking to win by foregrounding the economic risks
of independence. Journalist Ruth Wishart, speaking during the

referendum, saw this as characteristic of the general approach taken to the independence question:

> Many of the news based political editors seem to me just to have repeated whatever line they've been given by whatever new scare comes up and these ... seem to me to be given more prominence. There are countless examples in the last few weeks where, for instance an industrialist had said something positive about independence and it's an also ran on the politics pages. But if anybody bats an eyelid from the Better Together side from the business community, it's a splash, it's banner headlines, it's top of the page.

Scottish Labour's polling station posters, which bluntly proclaimed 'it's not worth the risk,' were the logical conclusion to a campaign that consistently emphasised financial and macro-economic questions that were often unanswerable in political terms. Such stories, particularly combined with market jitters as the polls narrowed, allowed large business organisations to create a climate heavy with the threat of job losses and capital flight. Many of the largest firms grouped together in the skittish but avowedly pro-union CBI, offered a concerted effort, through their own in-house public relations vehicles, to shape the news agenda. This notion, which at its most extreme was presented by the press as a very real and imminent danger of dire economic consequences, certainly demonstrates a failure on the part of journalistic inquiry. Yet given the rapid succession of announcements from corporate giants like John Lewis, Standard Life and BP in the final days leading up to the vote, it would have been extremely difficult for news gathering organisations to find the resources to probe successive claims as they were being made. Such warnings were bound to come into conflict with the kind of forward planning that coverage of major events always entails, arriving, as they did, in the final frenetic days of campaigning. In this manner the UK Government successfully orchestrated a campaign to make warnings about independence from a business perspective intensify at a crucial juncture. With the vote only days away, space to question these threats in the media was always going to be restricted, they also effectively by-passed 'purdah' rules that explicitly prevented civil servants making public statements at this time. The inescapable reality of capital flight, as in the *Financial Times* report that 'hundreds of millions of pounds were being pulled from Scotland' saw a torrent of coverage about economic risk dominate the media.[15]

Earlier, longer form analysis of the economics of independence as in Robert Peston's BBC documentary *For Richer for Poorer,* had offered a far more balanced picture. However, the issue at the crux of coverage of the economics of independence is not about the approach taken by top-flight editors. Rather, it is a question that resides with the often forgotten, but crucially important, newsroom staffers. The reporters whose job is not to shape, analyse, or comment upon a wider narrative, but to present, in the heat of the moment, in as representative a form as possible, the daily news agenda.

It is worth remembering that at its root media and the role it plays in our society is not about a vast conspiracy to shape an audience's views, nor is it a neutral vessel that simply acts as a conduit for information (though, confusingly, it can be capable of doing both). Rather, media is about representation. A kind of ongoing, multi-layered process of filtering and selection that makes its way to us in a variety of forms with the aim of representing to us what is actually happening. The nature of this process was succinctly described by Noam Chomsky and Edward S. Herman in their seminal work on media power in the United States, *Manufacturing Consent,*

The raw material of news must pass through successive filters, leaving only the cleansed residue fit to print. They fix the premises of discourse and interpretation, and the definition of what is newsworthy in the first place, and they explain the basis and operations of what amount to propaganda campaigns.[16]

Although this filtering process can never be neutral, it is extremely effective at taking on the semblance of neutrality, at constructing as 'facts' and 'news' that which is often fed into the media machine rather than gathered to it by intrepid journalistic effort. This is where media becomes politicised: the question of who selects what, and for whom, is critical. News has to be filtered, otherwise it would overwhelm us, that's a basic reality that we have to accept. Yet without an awareness of that process, as Chomsky and Herman explain, we risk forgetting how subtle and pervasive this filtering can be:

The elite domination of the media and marginalisation of dissidents that results from the operation of these filters occurs so naturally that media news people, frequently operating with complete integrity and goodwill, are able to convince themselves that they choose and interpret the news "objectively" and on the basis of professional news values. Within the limits of the filter's constraints they often are objective, the constraints are so powerful, and are built into the system in such a fundamental way, that alternative bases of news choices are hardly imaginable.[17]

This is why the structures that underpin the media are so important and can have a decisive impact on how stories are covered and wider narratives framed. This has become an increasingly topical issue at a UK level.

Money, Truth and Journalism

Peter Oborne stunned many of his colleagues when he took to the pages of *openDemocracy* to bemoan the editorial practices at the *Daily Telegraph* in February 2015. In an excoriating piece entitled 'Why I resigned from the *Telegraph'* Oborne revealed the extent to which commercial links to HSBC played a role in shaping editorial decisions at the paper, 'The *Telegraph's* recent coverage of HSBC' he stated, 'amounts to a form of fraud on its readers. It has been placing what it perceives to be the interests of a major international bank above its duty to bring the news to *Telegraph* readers.' The fraught issue of objectivity is as old as the profession of journalism itself. Yet despite all the pressures now facing the newspaper industry there is a stubborn, bloody-minded, sense of morality still prevalent amongst journalists. Elusive though its practice may be in this day and age, the notion of honest, factual reporting distinct from commentary as a public good, remains remarkably strong. As Oborne points out, 'A free press is essential to a healthy democracy. There is a purpose to journalism, and it is not just to entertain. It is not to pander to political power, big corporations and rich men. Newspapers have what amounts in the end to a constitutional duty to tell their readers the truth.' [18]

That duty is, in reality, a fairly subjective one. It would be impossible to prove that the Scottish press, reeling from the effects of its own corporate meltdown, was cowed by big business, or that its duty to rigorously report news was placed upon the altar of advertising revenue. However, what the overall picture of the coverage demonstrates is the extent to which forces representing the status quo, the establishment and large business interests, were not put under the same degree of scrutiny as those advocating change. Overwhelmingly support for Yes came not from large corporations, but from the small business sector: smaller organisations, far less able to effectively promote their messages in the press. The increasing influence of commercial factors over editorial decision making is personified for Oborne by 'the rise of shadowy executives who determine what truths can and what truths can't be conveyed across the mainstream media.' On top of that the increasing pursuit of 'clickbait' stories (often of dubious news value but more likely to boost online visits) has diluted the traditional core function of newspapers to report the most compelling or relevant facts of the day. As commentators were quick to point out in the wake of these revelations, the *Telegraph* has lost around half of its print sales over the last 10 years: far from being an organisation defined by an abstract constitutional duty, it is a commercial organisation, struggling to make a profit. Much like the *Scotsman*, using its 'Friends of the Scotsman' scheme to encourage organisations to take out a subscription in exchange for dedicated column inches, the commercial imperatives of the newspaper business are starting to crowd out journalistic values.[19]

While the challenge presented by the vast, complex and unpredictable referendum story was met with an inadequate response in Scotland's newsrooms, it doesn't take too much digging to comprehend why this was seen to be the case. That inadequacy was not the product of some vast unionist conspiracy. Instead, this major story arrived on news desks with all its strangeness and novelty at a time when Scottish journalism was less able to address it than it has been at any other point in its history. The reasons for this are complex, but one fairly clear issue that we can identify is the increasing pressure that journalism as a profession has been placed under in recent years. To work in a newsroom today is to work for longer hours, with less reward, while being expected to generate more content than ever before. In July 2015 the story of John Toner, a journalist on Newsquest's North London titles was illustrative of the extreme level of pressure the profession now faces. Toner explained that he was threatened with disciplinary procedures for not meeting his quota of filing six stories a day. In this instance he was unable to meet the quota as he was the only member of his family able to take his terminally ill grandmother to hospital. Despite this, he managed to file five stories on that day, but missing the quota by one still invoked the wrath of his employer, prompting Toner to resign.[20]

Though many journalists are reticent, for obvious reasons, about what has happened to their profession, discussion of its dire state are commonplace. From the trials of the honest hacks at the *Baltimore Sun* in HBO's epic of American decline, *The Wire,* to the National Theatre of Scotland's experimental theatrical exploration of the struggling trade, *The Enquirer,* tales of an increasingly fragile fourth estate and its arcane but charming rituals, quirks and principles, are widespread. In part this is a kind of radical nostalgia, for good times that were, at least in terms of salaries, profits and expense accounts, really good. Today, the largesse of once massively profitable enterprises has disappeared. In the face of private companies that long ago reconciled themselves to doing more with less, journalism is reeling, as the commercial funding that supports it has been holed below the waterline. Many media companies manage a vast portfolio of titles and are rarely capable of keeping their ear to the ground in terms of the specific needs of individual papers. The institution of the newsroom is increasingly under threat. On top of that, in the UK, 70% of national newspaper circulation is controlled by just three companies. A tendency in the newspaper market for large companies to swallow up vast portfolios of titles has led to increasing concerns that such concentration of ownership stifles plurality and hands excessive power to a tiny elite of proprietors, executives and editors.[21]

Background Stories

In Scotland the risks associated with these issues should not be underestimated. Increasing numbers of Scots have simply switched off from a media that they feel alienated from, with its obvious failure to reflect a political shift of epochal proportions. Major scandals such as phone hacking have also played a part in making the profession widely disdained in the popular imagination. A poll by Ipsos Mori published in January 2015 found that an astonishing 73% of respondents did not trust journalists to tell the truth. 'The ordinary man/woman in the street' was 40 points ahead of journalists in terms of how much they were trusted to tell the truth.[22]

If Leveson served to burst the bubble of Rupert Murdoch's almost shaman like charm with the UK political class, it also exposed journalism and its practices to public attention in a manner that is, in the UK at least, without precedent. The extreme views that the phone hacking scandal provoked were laden with concerns that the establishment response failed to speak to. In Scotland such disillusionment was all too easily refracted into a picture of amoral and venal hacks propping up the union and showing a distinct lack of enthusiasm for the idea that their notional readership might engage in a bit of old fashioned self-determination. When the referendum contest came round, an issue invoking passions and complexities that made it inherently challenging to cover, Scotland's fourth estate was in the worst possible position to offer an effective response. Unlike the BBC, who were handed additional resources from London: for the Scottish press, there was little or no recourse to a well-resourced network for help. In short, years of neglect by profit driven companies managing concerns openly struggling for commercial viability had come home to roost. In this context, the Scottish press's almost blanket unionism was as much a bitter footnote to its own drawn out death agony, as it was a principled defence of the old order.

At the same time, for all the popular disdain that has been heaped upon it, for many, journalism remains a sought after and prestigious career. As a result, a small number of precious internships at national titles are increasingly coveted, leading large news organisations to draw on a narrower group of wealthy graduate recruits. The now notorious intern culture within London media organisations serves to radically restrict the kind of backgrounds from which aspiring journalists are able to gain entry to the profession. The increasing prevalence of unpaid internships in media industries has had the effect of excluding candidates from poorer backgrounds: as a report from the Sutton Trust noted, 31% of internships are unpaid while the personal cost of taking on such a role in London amounts to £926 per month.[23] Research by the trust also found that over half of Britain's top 100 journalists are privately educated - even though just 7% of British pupils attended a private school.[24] In his book on the prevalence of class and privilege in the running of British institutions, *The Establishment,* Owen Jones describes an elitist 'mediaocracy' who wield extensive power through their position in the upper echelons of the UK press:

> The British people are not being served by a media that exists to inform them, to educate them, to understand the realities of the country they live in and the world around them. Instead much of the media is a political machine, lobbying for the often personal objectives of their owners. The media and political elites are frequently deeply intertwined, sharing as they do many of the same assumptions about how society should be run and organised. Journalists are often utterly subordinated to the whims of their editors, and increasingly drawn from backgrounds that are strikingly different from those of their readers.[25]

However much objectivity might be a widely held goal, journalists, like all writers, bring a set of values to approaching any story. While many aspire to look beyond them and achieve objectivity, there is an inevitable cultural and political imprint based on any writer's background and life experience. As Ian Bell points out, 'as in most things you start off with a group of people whose first loyalties are class loyalties, who, secondly, are not actually accustomed to questioning the status quo. There's almost an instinctive loyalty to the status quo.' Bell, a prominent advocate of left-wing politics in his columns for the *Herald* and *Sunday Herald*, notes how he has often struggled with the pervasiveness of class in framing how the media approaches certain stories, 'Scotland's media are still made by the middle class, for the middle class. Perspectives – we saw as much during the referendum – follow. I haven't lived in a housing scheme for a very long time, obviously. The voices still sit at the back of my head.'

Alongside the restricted opportunities for aspiring journalists, there is the increasingly problematic development of a professional caste of public relations experts and media managers, who work to constrain and direct media narratives. The most comprehensive study of the pressures this places on newsrooms was conducted by the University of Cardiff in 2008. Their report, *The Quality and Independence of British Journalism,* found that one in five stories were 'verifiably derived mainly or wholly from PR material or activity.' They also noted that journalists were, 'required to do more with less time, a trend that inevitably increases their dependence on "ready made" news and limits opportunities for independent journalism.' They found that journalists are expected to produce three times as much copy as they were twenty years ago.[26]

Such dependence on external sources for pre-packaged content is unlikely to lend itself to the kind of inquisitive practices that certain stories inevitably require. Disparagingly referred to as 'churnalism' such practices have the effect of inherently limiting the diversity of news stories, as multiple titles pick up copy from the same external sources, especially news agencies, to fill out column inches. The Cardiff report also found this to be a concern in both print and broadcast media, 'overall, our research suggests that 60% of press articles and 34% of broadcast stories come wholly or mainly from one of these "pre-packaged" sources.'

Partly drawing on this research, journalist Nick Davies conducted an extensive study into the nature of churnalism in his book *Flat Earth News*. Davies claims that media corporations now display a tendency to 'recycle ignorance,' due to the cuts imposed on newsrooms and that they have, 'slashed the old supply lines which used to fill up raw information from the ground; and, with the advent of news websites, added the new imperative of speed.' This, according to Davies creates 'news factory' conditions that have severely restricted the ability of journalists to investigate, chase a story, or find genuine scoops, 'Working in a news factory, without the time to check, without the chance to go out and make contacts and find leads, reporters are reduced to churnalism, to the passive processing of material which overwhelmingly tends to be supplied for them by outsiders, particularly wire and PR agencies.'[27] For Andrew Marr, this is a critical issue that the profession has to face up to:

> Office based journalists are vulnerable to the PR machines, the con-men, the special interest groups and above all errors that have been trapped in electronic or paper files. This is why so many papers, from the upmarket to the down market, carry the same stories, often treated in the same bland way...Journalism needs the unexpected. It needs the unpredictability and oddness of real life. That means it needs real reporters.[28]

The effect of such practices often stands in direct opposition to the public interest: particularly egregious examples of the combination of heavy PR and churnalism with regard to health have been debunked by doctor and journalist Ben Goldcare, for example.[29] Over the longer-term, such tendencies have the potential to damage the professional reputation of journalism even further, given that, in effect, it amounts to the privileging of particular agendas over public interest. Often these agendas will be expressed under the auspices of NGOs, think tanks and professional bodies. As a vast range of special interests wields increasing influence over the press and broadcasters, journalism risks the loss of its status as a 'public' function. The increasingly difficult task of filling a newspaper with a credible amount of material on a given day has destabilised the traditional liberal notion of a free, commercially driven, press as a natural means to hold the powerful to account. There has always been a tension between the dual role of newspapers as dissemina-tors of information to the public and as commercial organisations whose only real obligation is to shareholders and proprietors, but it has never been quite so acute.

The role that technology has played in this is critical. As we'll discuss later, there are countless examples of how digital tech-nology has revolutionised access to media, creating a culture of vibrant debate unprecedented since the days of the coffee houses and salons out of which the first newspapers in Western Europe emerged. Yet it has also proved a double-edged sword, eroding the income streams that underpinned quality journalism, but also fundamentally altering the kind of practices involved in news-gathering. The values of what many still feel is a noble profession have in effect been squeezed by two factors: on the one hand fewer resources as advertising revenue is monopolised by internet giants, and on the other an increasing reliance on digital technology to piece together stories remotely.

It is of course possible to interrogate and engage with a story from a remote location. But the warning remains a salient one. If journalism is now to be factory farmed, rather than afforded the freedom to roam, to discover and to report back, the quality of what news organisations are able to provide is bound to diminish over time. This is made even more problematic when we remember that journalists are increasingly drawn from elite backgrounds. Those already within the political and economic establishment are far more likely to have pre-existing relationships and to rely on a restricted pool of reliable and influential sources. In this depressingly narrow field, feedback loops become commonplace. The field also remains depressingly masculine, as the International Women's Media Federation pointed out in 2011, 'Taken together, UK news companies exhibit entrenched institutional practices of marginalizing women in their newsroom and decision-making hierarchies.'[30]

During the referendum, there was little incentive for overworked journalists to venture beyond the safe and reliable centres of mainstream political activity in Edinburgh, London and Glasgow (parliaments, press conferences, photo calls and so on). In contrast, Yes voters were predominantly found in less affluent parts of the country.[31] Such areas are marginalised in a number of different ways and are often quite literally switched off from the digital world, let alone part of any network of influence. Scotland's digital divide is acute – as of February 2015 a fifth of Scottish households had no internet access.[32] Given that existing journalistic networks have a scant relationship with such areas, engaging with low-income voices is inherently more time consuming and expensive. The Yes vote was obscured in the media, it could be argued, because it was harder to get to and lay largely beyond the milieu of most Scottish journalists.

Lesley Riddoch, reflecting on the BBC's coverage of the referendum, suggested that after years of justifying 'dull' and relatively narrow coverage of political issues in Scotland, the arrival of a story as vast and complex as the referendum amounted to a kind of culture-shock for some BBC staff:

> Lots of those guys in there, not all of them and that's the
> point, are just lazy. That's another very subjective thing

to say, but it's lazy not to keep your hand in and to know how society's changing. But they're part of a middle class ghetto that reinforces its own ideas very strongly. In the old days before mobile phones we had to get our butts out to stories. So you knew what people thought in the miner's strike, the Ravenscraig dispute or whatever, cause you had to physically go out and speak to them. Now that sort of exchange is relatively limited: so people just sit in buildings calling their existing contacts.

The notion that effective journalism involves getting out of the office and regular haunts in the world of politics and business is a noble aim. Given the current pressures placed on reporters, particularly when covering a story as fast moving as the referendum, output often consisted of lines that had been fed from politicians, business leaders, or other news outlets. For Neil Mackay, Editor of the *Sunday Herald*, the risks of such practices are clear:

If I see a reporter just sitting here in this office I go nuts, get out and talk to people, don't sit in this consensus middle class bubble. We're all middle class, we all went to good schools, we all went to good universities, we're all well paid, we can all sit here and we'll achieve nothing but an echo chamber of progressive middle class opinion.

Mackay's vehemence that journalism ought to be about stepping out of the office and into places where a journalist's natural comfort zone does not extend, contrasts with the reality of many modern newsrooms. This remains a live and controversial issue within the trade: as can be seen in the dispute focused on Trinity Mirror staff, adamant in their refusal to become 'click-bait' journalists.[33] While the *Sunday Herald* has bucked the trend and increased its sales since the referendum, the overall picture in the Scottish media says something far more troubling. Namely, just when Scotland needed the kind of active, inquiring 'old school journalism' that is explorative in its remit, many of Scotia's dwindling cohort of full time hacks were chained to their desks. If richer, more and more expansive coverage of the campaign was not wholly absent, it certainly wasn't the norm.

In a newspaper market that still sees up to half of all newspapers in the UK chasing an essentially middle class readership, wealthier, elite voices have far more opportunity to have their case made in the media than less well off members of society. As James Curran and Jean Seaton explain, 'quality newspapers were protected from the economic pressure to build large circulation because over two-thirds of their revenue came from advertising secured by reaching small, elite audiences.'[34] The will to deviate from the instinctive hostility of middle Scotland to independence was, perhaps inevitably, largely absent from the pages of Scotland's broadsheet titles, cowed as these papers were by years of internal instability and cuts.

Often, broadcasters such as Channel 4 faired far better at delving into the many individual and collective stories that made up the independence issue. The value of the reporter on the spot is something that many veteran journalists are fond of extolling. Few have done so more eloquently than Jon Snow, who has written of the risks that stem from journalism that is not given licence to roam:

Technology has given us the wonder of instant, the knowledge of the suffering now, but not what it means human to human. Technology has given us the global village of images ready to weave into as comprehensive an account as mankind has ever known. We have invested in technology. But we have neglected the human. We have danced to the music of endless pictorial options. We have dispatched willing writers to editing devices to wax poetic about scenes they have often seen but rarely, if ever, witnessed … the homogenised images are a vital concomitant, they are not the core. The core is the human, the reporter as witness. And despite the brilliance and the comprehensiveness of the global village, nothing has replaced her or him.[35]

Snow has also described the current era as a 'golden age of journalism' recognising the opportunities that sit alongside the risks of digital technology.[36] But there is a crucial point that underlies his tribute to the journalist in the field: it costs money, lots of money, the kind of sums of money increasingly unavailable to any media outlet in Scotland. It is hard to find an experienced journalist who will not bemoan current levels of staffing and resources. The most fundamental role of the reporter: to witness and interpret the experience of other human beings, really has become an infrequent, almost arcane pursuit in Scotland. This is a matter of national concern – to which the abrasive form of disconnect that developed between media and audience during the referendum bears testament.

Conclusion

Despite all the evidence that journalism as a profession is increasingly struggling for viability, there is widespread inertia in the UK about what can be done about this issue. Scotland, as we will see in the next chapter, has had to contend with the narrow output of a diminished media in a manner that has had obvious and damaging results. The real nature of this issue is about the eroding of public interest as the basic test of journalistic value. How might media in Scotland begin to develop the kind of structures that value diversity of content, background and ownership? There are multiple points that we could start from. Post Collective's Lee Bunce, who takes inspiration from the world of academic research, has shown how public funding can be divorced from any form of political interference, through explicit commitments to independence, public interest and publishing under open licence.[37] It is also widely accepted in Scotland that the arts receive public funds and while the institutions and structures that make this possible are far from perfect, the principle is well established.

There are also interesting innovations taking place within magazine journalism. International titles like *Monocle, Colors, N+1* and *Jacobin*, have thrived at harnessing the power of subscriptions to refashion successful independent long form journalism and offer high production values. Another magazine emblematic of this revival, *Delayed Gratification,* prides itself on promoting 'slow journalism.' Print is able to regain readership by offering an immersive, reflective experience, as the pace of digital media becomes overwhelming. As it happens, a Scottish foray into this world is already underway. According to its Elgin based founder Alex MacLeod, *Grapevine* is premised on 'taking the experience of reading a really good global magazine, and putting that design and editorial ethos to work on intelligent local content.' MacLeod is confident that print journalism in Scotland is ready for such a shake up as quality and variety declines elsewhere, 'For print to thrive, it needs to return to its analytical, reflective roots ... What Scottish dailies need to do for an engaged, disenchanted reader like me is to offer the immersive experience that digital can never hope to replicate.' It is perhaps intriguing that *Grapevine* – aimed at offering a Highland audience a media product that links in with urban, global culture – is one of a very small number of media start-ups in Scotland with a solid commercial plan. In fact, the state of the local press in Scotland, dominated by the Scottish Provincial Press and Johnston Press, is increasingly drab and devoid of life. Perhaps a revival of Scottish journalism and the search for new mechanisms to support it could start at a local level.

There is a precedent for effective state subsidy to promote this. Sweden's system of press funding, based on a three per cent advertising levy, has served to rebalance the country's regional press against the dominance of metropolitan media. In the UK, London based titles account for 75% of all sales, in Sweden, papers based in Stockholm have only a third of the market.[38] Of course, such a progressive move took place after a long debate in the 1960s with parallel changes in Norway and Denmark. It was premised on widespread fears about the erosion of national media in a country already independent with its own written constitution. Yet the debate on Scotland's media too often focuses on the national titles, if journalism were to be revived north of the border, starting at a regional level makes sense. With titles like the Dundee *Courier* and Aberdeen's *Press and Journal* now outselling the *Scotsman* and the *Herald*, this kind of strategy to support journalism could also be inherently sustainable. The funding of independent journalistic ventures could be based around a New Media Trust aimed at supporting new media start-ups with resources, mentoring and advice. A healthy and decentralised media is, by definition, far less likely to become the domain of group-think and powerful agendas. However, the question of Scotland's democratic media deficit cannot simply be addressed at a grassroots level. The structures that are supposed to provide diversity in Scotland's national media remain inadequate. To understand the scale of this problem, we have to go back and consider how the Scottish referendum was covered and why the role of the Scottish media in the debate became so fiercely contested.

2

Ten Days to Save Britain

Robin McAlpine, a former journalist and now director of left-wing 'think and do' tank, Common Weal, was unequivocal about the underlying issue at the heart of how the media dealt with the referendum story:

> The biggest problem with the media in Scotland today is that it's falling apart … We have one of our two main broadsheet newspapers that no longer employs a photographer. We have another newspaper in Scotland which is supposed to be a serious national newspaper which is put together by the sorts of numbers of journalists that … you'd call it a fanzine. That's the fundamental problem. It's collapsing … a collapsing, dying entity has just become really bad.

While much of the Yes campaign was organised at a community level, it was overwhelmingly outgunned in terms of prominent establishment organisations who were prepared to use their leverage to develop a pro-union narrative that could be packaged and re-presented by the media. 'There are a number of, what I would call, organising mechanisms for the British establishment in Scotland, and they are operating in very particular ways,' says McAlpine, 'They are coordinating their messages … you have things like the David Hume Institute or the Royal Society of Edinburgh who have been very good at organising the British establishment in Scotland and you've got most of the newspapers who are doing much the same thing,' he adds.

This view was also expressed during the referendum campaign by Ruth Wishart who noted, '...maybe people think that if they take information from a certain establishment source it must be okay, it must be true, it must be tablets of stone and if they take that information from a less well established source ... they give that less weight perhaps.' For Neil Mackay, such an approach is also about marginalising 'radical voices':

> What I feel is wrong in journalism and political culture full stop across the United Kingdom is this status quo consensus, and I see it all the time: where a radical voice is often ridiculed, mocked, sidelined, portrayed as somehow from a loony fringe, when that doesn't happen in other countries ... But yes, I just feel it's a kind of status quo consensus and it's idle journalism.

During the referendum, establishment sources were overwhelmingly found on one side of the debate. This single factor was at the heart of a prevalent bias against independence. Most notably of all, the CBI entered the debate as a proponent of the union by registering with the Electoral Commission as an official campaign. In response several prominent organisations including Scottish universities and STV left the organisation, while others, like the BBC, suspended their membership until the end of the referendum campaign. While the CBI successfully deregistered itself (citing an administrative error) after seeking to clarify its role as a business rather than a political organisation, it continued to make announcements in the run up to the referendum.[39] On 28 August, for example, its president Sir Mike Rake remarked 'The risks of a Yes vote for Scotland and the UK are enormous.'[40]

The BBC's Scotland Correspondent, James Cook, felt that there was a legitimate concern about how rigorously the status quo was questioned by the media. Speaking to *aPolitical* podcast in July 2015 he remarked:

> ...people live in the status quo, so you can understand the notion that the obsession is with the unknown – could the media have done more to really get under the kind of, where we are in Scotland, Britain and where we are heading, is this a good thing if we remain in the union? I think probably they could have, actually, to be honest with you, and I wouldn't like that to be seen as a partisan point. I have no axe to grind on one side of this campaign or the other ... I think there's a case that you could have done a bit more digging about the society we live in, where we're heading.

If a frail Scottish journalism was vulnerable to the influence of large, well-funded, corporate organisations, the inevitable pressure applied by party spin-doctors was also significant. This two way process served to keep the debate within confines that the media could recognise in order to view the debate as essentially a party political matter. Political coverage is often far cheaper and more streamlined if it is reduced to a bi-partisan contest. *Scotland Tonight's* leaders debates, which pitted Deputy First Minister Nicola Sturgeon against a succession of pro-union politicians, were a somewhat overblown example of this tendency. Complete with ringside pundits at half time, bizarre technological gimmicks such as a 'word cloud', and a non-discursive format, they managed to offer remarkably little insight about the wider debate, while any points raised were lost in a succession of public displays of animosity.

As the story developed, coverage of the referendum became defined by such media spectacles. John Mullin, who headed the BBC's referendum unit, cited a debate at the SSE Hydro with 8,000 first time voters as the jewel in the crown of the BBC's coverage,

'Who else would even have tried to pull that one off? That programme is the very definition of public sector broadcasting at its very best.'[41] However it was the two debates between First Minister Alex Salmond and Better Together Campaign Chairman Alistair Darling that provided the main focal points in the media account of the referendum. While they attracted massive viewings figures, they also served to shift the parameters of the debate away from the streets and communities of Scotland and into the confines of televisual formats that could be easily managed and would generate multiple stories off the back of one event.[42] Democratic Audit UK, analysing Twitter responses to both the Salmond-Darling contest and the 'town hall' style debate screened on STV on 2 September (with three panellists from different backgrounds on each side) found that audiences engaged more positively with the latter format, noting:

> The sample tweets were generally critical of the behaviour exhibited during the first two events, with many linking this to the debates' all-male formats. As one Twitter user observed, this demonstrated 'macho politics at its worst'. In contrast, the composition of the town hall debate panel (six debaters, of which four were women) was seen largely by the Twitter audience as having contributed to a far more positive viewing experience.[43]

A big disparity between the two campaigns was to be found in their composition. Largely the domain of party activists and employees on the Better Together side, Yes was defined primarily by its spontaneous, grassroots, character. The former were always on the end of a phone and could feed crucial information to journalists, the latter were so numerous and multifarious that they could provide neither. All that could be offered was a narrative that did not fit with the soundbites and messaging that were reliably available from party and campaign HQs. For some this tendency was exemplified when a notable exception to party-centric coverage, the popular Sunday morning review on BBC Scotland, *Headlines*, was replaced by *Crossfire*. *Headlines*, presented by Ken MacDonald, had offered a broader view of the political scene in Scotland and made a point of quoting blogs and other alternative media while discussing a wide range of issues. Its replacement, a format designed to give equal airtime to two party-political co-presenters, seemed a retrograde step.[44] Drawing on his own experience within the corporation, Yes Scotland Chief Executive Blair Jenkins claims it was a party-centric mentality that often made the BBC oblivious, until very late in game, about what was taking place on the ground, 'Because its own funding and its own future depends so heavily on political parties, I think the BBC more than other broadcasters took a party political view of the referendum. So in essence they saw it as a competition between politicians. And that wasn't the campaign we were running.'

The Enemy Within

The tendency to represent a political cause primarily through party political channels is perhaps best exemplified by a focus on leadership: the attributes and failings of individuals fronting a certain position. It is inherently easier for news organisations to focus on leaders and media personalities rather than a diverse range of voices and perspectives that support a certain position. The most obvious case in point was the manner in which Alex Salmond became the personification of the independence issue. The resulting sustained negative focus on the leader of a movement has not been seen in the British media since Arthur Scargill's leadership of the National Union of Mineworkers. Like Scargill, Salmond was frequently portrayed as a vainglorious and dangerous demagogue. As a means to keep the focus of coverage constrained, such personification allowed a whole movement to be reduced to one man's personal ambition and hubris. Salmond, notoriously fond of political confrontation, has for some time been the Scottish press corps favoured bête noire, not least due to his ability to bounce back throughout a long political career. On top of that, he has led a remarkably disciplined SNP that seems immune to the kind of intrigues and personality clashes that afflict other mainstream parties. Headlines such as 'Salmond's Black Wednesday' (*Daily Record*), 'Salmond accused of bullying top academic' (*Telegraph*) and 'Tirade of hate that shames Salmond' (*Mail*) became typical as the campaign began to heat up. David Patrick of the University of the Free State conducted a content analysis of front-page articles, editorials and comment pieces in eight Scottish newspapers between September 2013 and March 2014. He found that of 57.2% of all occasions where someone's name was in the headline of the article, that name was Alex Salmond.[45]

This willingness by the media to use one man's profile as short hand for the independence movement aligned neatly with Better Together's campaign language, which deliberately set out to characterise all independence supporters as members of the SNP, to ignore the grassroots support for Yes and to suggest that control was entirely vested in the First Minister himself. At points the campaign spilled into demonisation: including references to Salmond's marriage, 'Childless SNP chiefs "who have no feel for UK family"' ran one *Daily Mail* headline.[46] Far from being a pro-union campaign, Better Together often seemed to be, in essence, an anti-Salmond one. In part this was due to the lack of a single, popular and charismatic leader to front the No offer. Well-liked figures such as Charles Kennedy and Annabelle Goldie were courted to take on leadership roles, but declined. As a long running spat over who would debate who revealed, the Better Together side were reluctant to have the campaign associated with David Cameron, or any frontline politician (despite the fact that many did, nonetheless, take part in eleventh hour engagements on the campaign trail). As John Robertson noted in his controversial content analysis of BBC and STV programming, the personalisation of the campaign was a critical tool in allowing Yes to be undermined:

> Personalisation of political issues is a long-established strategy to weaken arguments, shifting focus from collective reasoning or shared values to supposed personal desires and personality traits ... The tendency by opposition politicians to attempt to undermine the Yes campaign by labelling its ambitions as Alex Salmond's desires is, in part, beyond the editorial role, however, it was common for reporters and presenters to adopt the same style.[47]

The task of translating a big tent movement that was in many ways the successor of various protest movements (against the Iraq War, Trident and the Poll Tax for example) was always bound to be less media savvy than the more focused, party political campaign that advocated union. In fact, many of the challenges that the Yes campaign confronted in the media were similar to those faced by the anti-war movement in 2003. As protesters at the time noted, this was often characterised by the BBC attempting to achieve 'balance' by always having a pro-war voice to match an anti-war voice in its coverage. 'The war exposed a serious disconnection between the political elite and the public,' reflected David Miller in 2003, 'so the usual method of ensuring "balance" - interviewing politicians - was never going to be enough.' This narrow approach to balance took little account of the fact that there was no mass demonstration in favour of the war and that a sizeable chunk of the British press, including all of Murdoch's newspapers, and indeed the machinery of government itself, stood behind Tony Blair's case for invasion. As with the referendum, the support of both governing and opposition parties for the war meant that the traditional means of achieving balance were unavailable to the BBC and they proved more reluctant than other broadcasters to innovate on this front.[48] In relation to the war itself, David Edwards and David Cromwell of *Media Lens* described 'The Bias In BBC "Balance"', concluding, 'The BBC does occasionally provide space for dissident opinions, but these are vanishingly rare moments of honesty swamped by an overwhelming pro-establishment bias.'[49]

The definitive activities of social movements like Yes: the occupation of urban spaces through marches, public meetings, rallies and sit-ins, are rarely covered in any depth by mainstream media. If they're covered at all, there is a tendency to represent events as disorderly. As Tony Benn pointed out after student protest in 2011, protest is often ignored by the media unless it can be portrayed as an inherently violent activity.[50] The peaceful nature of Yes campaign marches, in September 2012, September 2013 and later rallies in Glasgow's George Square, meant that they drew minimal media attention. The lack of such displays of mass mobilisation in favour of the union presented a clear disparity. BBC Scotland's report on the 2013 pro-independence march and rally resorted to achieving 'balance' by giving the presence of less than ten Better Together canvassers out in Edinburgh equivalence with an event that drew tens of thousands.[51]

During any moment of acute and sustained political drama: industrial disputes, in the face of radical governments, or during moments of political crisis such as the Iraq War, the BBC, tied by its duty to be impartial and linked to millions of citizens via their licence fees, faces regular controversy over its coverage. In 2014 the Scottish referendum was not the only issue that saw protests outside the corporation's buildings. Its coverage of the Israeli bombardment of Gaza in June also drew angry crowds to its premises. Professor Greg Philo of the Glasgow Media Group commented on the *Today* programme as hundreds of protestors gathered outside New Broadcasting House: 'Many times senior journalists at the BBC have told me they simply cannot get the Palestinian viewpoint across … The Palestinian perspective is just not there.'[52] Looking back on the referendum Tariq Ali bemoaned the role of, 'The neutered BBC that during crises at home (Scotland) and wars abroad (Gaza, Iraq, Syria, Afghanistan) is little more than a propaganda outfit.'[53] Though he would later refuse to elaborate further on his remark, Channel 4's Paul Mason quipped on Facebook, 'Not since Iraq have I seen BBC News working at propaganda strength like this. So glad I'm out of there.'[54]

The inability of the BBC to grasp the nature of the Yes movement would have been less controversial had one of its first reports on the non-party aspect of the debate not consisted of an 'exclusive' from Gavin Esler on a blatantly astroturfed campaign by Tory donor and millionaire Malcolm Offord. Called Vote No Borders, a subsequent puff piece on BBC News 24 focused on its attempt to create 'a grassroots campaign to rival that of the pro-independence Yes campaign.' The issue of the lack of emotion and passion in the official pro-union campaign had been raised, particularly within the Scottish Conservative party, for some time. By March 2014 'there had been debates for months about whether Better Together needed to be more positive.'[55] The apparent willingness of BBC editors to help resolve the No campaign's issues by presenting a unionist marketing venture (led and funded by a millionaire) as a grassroots initiative provoked criticism and derision on social media. This was made all the more poignant given that the basic facts about Vote No Border's corporate origins were easily accessible online. The manner in which the report was framed was telling:

With the No campaign being criticised by supporters for a lacklustre performance compared to the fiery campaigning of Scotland's First Minister Alex Salmond and his supporters, now BBC News has learned of an alternative No campaign which calls itself 'No Borders', a group determined to rouse the emotions many feel about being Scottish and British.[56]

The Vote No Borders case illustrates two of the most important issues about the need for a better media in Scotland. On the one hand, it showed just how much the BBC was unable to get to grips with a new kind of movement politics on the Yes side, while also demonstrating, with quite alarming clarity, how an obviously 'pre-packaged' story could be presented as straight reportage. The falsehood was twofold: it was not only presented as objective news, but also a significant scoop. The fact that Vote No Borders was to become the object of ridicule and scandal (including a notorious run in with Great Ormond Street Hospital about specialist care for children post independence that saw one of its cinema adverts withdrawn) shows just how poor the BBC's judgement could be when covering the debate.[57]

Fear and News Values

In 1996 the French philosopher Pierre Bourdieu delivered a series of controversial lectures later published in the volume *On Television*. The book introduces the notion that journalists work in a 'field' that necessarily skews their approach and shapes their values, especially with regards to political discourse. The result is both the kind of narrowness and insularity described above and a self-serving desire to compete for audiences:

Because they're so afraid of being boring, they opt for confrontations over debates, prefer polemics over rigorous argument, and in general, do whatever they can to promote conflict. They prefer to confront individuals (politicians in particular) instead of confronting their arguments, that is, what's really at stake in the debate, whether the budget deficit, taxes, or the balance of trade. Given that their claims to competence are based more on their claims to close contacts in the political realm, including access to insider information (even rumours and malicious gossip), than on the objectivity of their observation and investigation, journalists like to stick to their home territory.[58]

In a sense, Bourdieu's point about how the media operates in relation to politics is a perfect description of how referendum coverage failed, in the first instance, to pick up on the broader and more eclectic aspects of the story, while also gesturing towards a wider point about how such habits can have a real and often malign impact on the quality of public debate. Bourdieu even goes so far as to claim that the desire to constantly catch the attention of citizens can result in the media shaping events themselves, through crass nationalist rhetoric, as exemplified in the escalation of a dispute between Turkey and Greece in December 1995, noting 'these nationalistic outbursts - in Turkey and Greece, but also in the former Yugoslavia, in France and elsewhere - may well lie in the ways modern media are able to exploit these primal passions.'[59]

The media, though it often characterises itself as performing a representative, analytical and reflective function, is often capable of becoming an actor in shaping events based on how it decides to treat a story. This is something that the British media is by no means immune from. An obvious case in point is the extensive coverage given to Anjem Choudary and his announcement of a plan to protest in Wootton Bassett in 2010. As Mehdi Hassan pointed out at the time, 'Our sensationalist and irresponsible media has, in fact, been deeply complicit in the rise and rise of this fanatic, devoting quite disproportionate and counter-productive coverage to his various rantings.'[60] Outrage is cheap, easily manufactured and can often sustain a story, such as that of Choudary's activities, simply on the basis that its offensiveness will generate not only a large audience, but also a means to keep the story running long after its original news value has been exhausted. The more recent appearance of Choudary on Fox News (he has also appeared on numerous flagship UK programmes such as the BBC's News-night, HARDtalk, and ITV's GMTV) is a testament to the manner in which media often devote disproportionate attention to fringe elements and extremists who are not in any way representative of a particular issue or community.[61]

As news media are increasingly called upon to improvise and keep a story moving, particularly via the 'switch off and you'll miss something' format of rolling news, it becomes all too easy for outlets to revert to pre-established narratives and confirmation bias. One clear example of this was rolling news coverage of the 2011 Norway attacks, where the lack of factual information about an unexpected and complex terrorist event resulted in widespread speculation and an assumption that the attacks must have been the result of a jihadist group such as Al-Qaeda. The *Sun*, anxious not to miss a beat, penned a reactionary editorial and printed a front page describing 'Norway's 9/11' as an 'Al-Qaeda massacre'.[62] As Chris Abbott, of the think tank Open Briefing reflected, '... preju-dice and inaccurate conjecture can be allowed to fill the space left vacant by fact – particularly on the rolling news channels, which stays with a story as it develops but often with very little other than opinion to report.'[63]

Allowing stories to be reported with only limited verifiable facts underpinning them is tied up with the tropes and character-istics of rolling news services, originally made possible thanks to the development of satellite communications in the second half of the twentieth century. This technological development meant that news could travel across the globe faster than ever before, later the rolling news format was pioneered by CNN during the first Gulf War. At the outset of the conflict in 1990 CNN had fewer than a million viewers: by its close, it had nearly seven million.[64] Trailers for the service were opportunistic in exploiting the rapid pace and excitement of conflict:

> As the ugly threat of war casts shadows on the gulf, there is one source, where President Bush checks Saddam Hussein's next move and Kuwait's royal family gets news from home, where families of hostages and servicemen learn about loved ones and King Hussein turns to offer peaceful resolution, where Iraq monitors UN sanctions and world reaction. The one source of information that these people have is the source you have, 24 hours a day, CNN.[65]

Here the medium itself is presented as a kind of gladiatorial arena. Not just helping to shape events but acting as the centre of the action: where the conflict would be planned, monitored, fought out, and resolved. It was offering viewers a sense that, by using this media product, they too would become as invested as the key players in the drama. Across rolling news services the use of ticker banners, visually compelling graphics to underline 'breaking news' and live coverage, two way exchanges with reporters 'at the scene' and the aggregation of content from smartphones and social media, serves to create a form of consuming news that rarely affords us the space to understand, digest or properly analyse the impact of events. The cynical use of such devices to keep an audience's attention inherently favours certain news values over others, with more dramatic and gripping coverage making it to the top of the bulletin. The actress Tilda Swinton has noted how this can cut both ways, 'the systematic amping up of the high drama of daily life as disseminated via the 'reality' of news programming must only key up a population to expect and need the adrenaline rush of sensational, result-heavy, political action from its leaders – its new bedtime storytellers.' [66] This blurring, as Bourdieu claims, leads to a situation in which media shapes politics and events in its own image, 'One thing leads to another, and, ultimately, television, which claims to record reality, creates it instead.'[67] As Neil Postman points out, the overall effect is to encourage media consumers to constantly await the next story or major development, rather than to stop, discuss, or consider the impact of events, 'There is no murder so brutal, no earthquake so devastating, no political blunder so costly - for that matter, no ball score so tantalising or no weather report so threatening - that it cannot be erased from our minds by a newscaster saying "now this."'[68]

Of course providers such as the BBC do offer opportunities for thought, investigation and analysis in their schedules. But like every other provider, when it moves into crisis mode, it becomes easily entangled in the action itself. Critical distance is easily lost in the face of a rapidly developing story that it must constantly keep pace with. This concern is also about how the story is framed and the kind of news values that are brought to bear upon it. While journalists do not think uniformly within a single organisation, the process of deciding what is newsworthy can be attributed to a set of broadly understood news values. In 1973 John Galtung and Marie Ruge identified eight universal news values, still relevant today:

- **Frequency**: does the event's time span fit with daily or weekly deadlines?

- **Amplitude**: how noticeable is the event, is it large scale enough to warrant coverage?

- **Clarity**: is the event clear-cut enough to be easily interpreted and understood?

- **Cultural proximity**: is the event relevant to the audience?

- **Predictability**: does it fit with the audience's expectations, prejudices or beliefs?

- **Unexpectedness**

- **Continuity**: is the story likely to run on and offer more opportunities for coverage?

- **Composition**: does the story fit as part of the wider mix of news being presented in a bulletin? [69]

Though they may not be identical to those listed above, not least because different editors will try and emphasise values that they think correspond to their own audiences, all news gathering operations weigh up the inherent attributes of any story against a list of criteria. Beyond simply making a story stand up, the task of a journalist is to establish what events are newsworthy: like medics at a triage station assessing the wounded most in need of treatment. A basic level of confusion in this process in relation to coverage of the referendum probably stemmed from the bland nature of standard news fare in Scotland. When London switched on to the debate in the final weeks, it panicked: historically stories about Scotland only rarely become matters of international interest. Scotland's broadcast news coverage is often criticised for being parochial and focused on court cases, vehicular accidents, and violent crime. While the reasons for this are complicated (and will be addressed in the next chapter) the set of news values at play within Scotland are not aligned to stories of 'national' (UK) import. The structure of UK news, as Brian McNair argues, has long played a role in shaping how judgements about news value are made:

The inevitable metro-centrism of media workers in the London area, meant that before devolution Scotland rarely appeared in the UK media in anything other than the most dreadful or dramatic contexts - the Ibrox disaster, the Piper Alpha disaster, the Dunblane massacre. After devolution, this pattern of coverage continued.[70]

Respondents to the 2008 Scottish Broadcasting Commission from the Children's Parliament and the Scottish Youth Parliament were acutely aware of this. 'If people not from Scotland were watching the news they would think it was terrible and scary,' observed one, 'Bad news is often reported more than good', said another. These young Scots picked up on the gulf in news values too, 'Scottish news is generally rather trivial, and cutting the normal news off in the middle to tell us there is a cat stuck up a tree in Lanarkshire is just annoying. Telling us about important news and specifically Scottish legislation is one thing. Cats are another.'[71]

But the prevalence of negative stories about Scotland, both before, during, and after the referendum, is not just a Scottish problem. Negative stories are, in a sense, far more likely to be gripping, dramatic, unexpected and easily packaged. In contrast, stories that are positive tend to be less so, a useful example is provided by Paul Hodkinson:

...gradual improvements in a country's education system are unlikely to make the news, unless highlighted by a discrete event, such as the release of a report or a high-profile school visit by a member of the government. Similarly, the slow process of repairing a war-torn country is liable to receive less coverage than the bombing that damaged it. The rebuilding of Lebanon in the 1990s and the early 2000s, for example, was ignored by the Western media until the project was set back by the discrete, short-term event of Israel bombing the country in 2006.[72]

In this sense, the 'bias' towards the Yes campaign was less to do with structural bias and more a particular kind of confirmation bias that was reflective of the starkly contrasting nature of the different campaigns. The messaging promoted by Yes Scotland was almost invariably positive, focusing on slow burning stories like the strength and diversity of the Scottish economy, the competence of the Scottish Government, the country's green energy potential and so on. In contrast Better Together's now notorious 'Project Fear' had a thrust that was far more translatable into news copy. Messaging from Yes was also predominantly centre-left in tone. As AA Gill remarked in *The Times*, 'the left-wing tends to care most about things it has managed to make a difference to, things that tend not to be hard news, but social engineering.'[73] Whether we like it or not 'risk' is inherently more newsworthy than 'opportunity' and the prospect of steep decline far more compelling than steady reform. The basic democratic argument at the heart of Yes, that Scotland should 'always get the government it votes for,' was by its very nature not going to change, develop or become imbued with a sense of urgency as the campaign wore on. In contrast, stories like Scotland's ability to form a Sterling Zone after independence involved several dramatic interventions from leading politicians and the Governor of the Bank of England. Big issues flagged by Yes Scotland, meanwhile, such as the removal of Trident, became far more easily caught up in competing narratives about membership of NATO that could be exploited, as in remarks by Lord George Robertson, to play on fears about global security. Above all, as Campaign Director of Better Together Blair MacDougall pointed out well before polling day, the campaign to save the UK was confident, based on its own data, that economic uncertainty would undermine the case for independence.[74] Independence, an unknown, was a proposition to be refuted, in contrast to the apparent stability represented by the UK. The No campaign was almost always in a commanding position from the get go and was far more successful at delivering a hard political message through the media based on a succession of short term, negative, but often dramatic, stories.

The link between the impact of fear on news values, and within the media more generally, on people's sense of security and agency has been a matter of some controversy amongst media scholars. Among the most prominent theories about how media can impact on individual's sense of political agency and social cohesion, is an oft-cited study by George Gerbner. It found that the effects of consuming large amounts of television tend to foster negative perceptions of the world:

> If you are growing up in a home where there is more than say three hours of television per day, for all practical purposes you live in a meaner world - and act accordingly - than your next-door neighbour who lives in the same world but watches less television. The programming reinforces the worst fears and apprehensions and paranoia of people.

Gerber also points out that this 'mean world syndrome' often 'results in a reduced sensitivity to the consequences of violence along with an increased sense of vulnerability and dependence – and therefore a demand for repression from the government.' Crucially, Gerbner sees direct political implications from these findings, 'It's impossible to run an election campaign without advocating more jails, harsher punishment, more executions, all the things that have never worked to reduce crime but have always worked to get votes. It's driven largely, although not exclusively, by television-cultivated insecurity.'[75] Fear and negativity are at home in the wider media landscape and in the referendum campaign they flourished. Data from Lord Ashcroft's poll on 18 September found 47% of No voters cited 'the risk of independence looked too great' as the most important reason for backing the union, a full 20 points ahead of the other reasons offered.[76] Given the tenor of the media debate in the final phase of the campaign, it's not hard to see why.

A 'Nation Divided'

On 7 September a YouGov poll predicted a 51% Yes vote. In doing so it drastically increased the news value of the referendum. As the *Guardian* would later describe it, the result was that, 'the referendum finally became a story of global proportions.'[77] YouGov's rounds of polling from 2-17 September showed the gap between Yes and No close markedly: recording at least 48% support for independence in this period, after excluding undecided voters.[78] As many Yes insiders would later attest, the headline poll on the 7 September was too soon, offering as it did the opportunity for the No campaign to galvanise its base and regroup. As Blair MacDougall recalled, 'Those two YouGov polls were the best thing that happened to the campaign in terms of making the economic risk real, in terms of energising activists and getting the parties to work through the painful process of sorting out this stuff.'[79]

Dire warnings about the effects of such a result, channelled through the UK government from big business, became dominant news stories from the 7 September onwards. Companies such as Standard Life, John Lewis, BP, RBS, Lloyds and Asda either announced or re-iterated fears about the risks and costs of independence. Much of this activity from the corporate sector was coordinated by a 'call to arms' from David Cameron on 11

September, as the *Financial Times* reported, the Prime Minister 'evoked Britain's defeat of Hitler in the second world war as he spoke to an audience of more than 100 business leaders of the need to fight to keep the UK together.' One chief executive said of the speech, 'He left us in no doubt that he thought we should speak out.'[80] In this period of intensive campaigning activity, of claim and counter claim, all the broad issues identified above came home to roost. The *Guardian's* succinct front page headline on its Scottish edition of 11 September, 'Banks: we'll leave if vote is Yes', was typical of the thrust of much of the coverage. Regardless of the details, Yes would bring negative and unquantifiable economic consequences in its wake.

This led to widely reported comments by Alex Salmond that 'whipped up metropolitan media coverage' had translated into bias against the Yes campaign, adding, 'I'm not really laying this charge at BBC Scotland. I just think metropolitan BBC has found this whole thing extraordinarily difficult, to separate their own view of the world from their view reporting Scotland.'[81] As several journalists gleefully reported Salmond's opinion on the coverage, the impression that the Yes campaign was 'under fire' became an increasingly prevalent part of the overall narrative. Salmond's press conference showdown with Nick Robinson, coupled with a third protest against BBC bias at Pacific Quay, sustained a narrative that events were moving beyond the pale.

As shares in Scottish companies tumbled, the BBC's Assistant Political Editor Norman Smith described the political drama from Edinburgh to viewers of BBC News 24 on 11 September, a week before the vote:

> ... it just gives you a sense of how extraordinarily charged this whole campaign has become and into which, bluntly, the BBC and what Mr Salmond calls the "metropolitan media" has been dragged ... Let me suggest also that

> Mr Salmond is perhaps not too discomforted by this row because it enables him to present himself as the underdog standing up to the Westminster politicians, who he accuses of bullying tactics and also standing up to what he regards as an over-mighty London media.[82]

But it was bullying of another sort that was to form another strong theme in coverage of the final days of the campaign. Given that the history of Scottish nationalism has been overwhelmingly peaceful and non-violent, there were bound to be limits to any efforts, beyond those of the characteristically rabid *Daily Mail*, to smear it as ethnic in origin and extremist in character. Despite this, a desire to paint the referendum as divisive and verging on violently confrontational can be seen in much of the coverage of the final days. One incident of criminality, involving an egg in Kirkcaldy, proved enough to draw significant press attention to what was clearly a marginal issue. In remarks which ran on a front page story in the *Herald* under the headline, 'Warning of polling station clashes as tensions rise', one Better Together source went as far as to warn of 'absolute carnage' on polling day. [83] In an unprecedented move, the Scottish Police Federation responded with a statement condemning those using 'intemperate, inflammatory and exaggerated language, lest they be seen to seek to create a self fulfilling prophecy.'[84]

The story originated in photo calls organised by future Scottish Labour leader Jim Murphy, who carried out a tour of Scotland on top of two Irn Bru crates, often provoking confrontations with Yes supporters. The tour was dramatically called off due to 'intimidation' when Murphy was egged in Kirkcaldy by Yes supporter Stuart Mackenzie, who was later sentenced to eighty hours of community service. As a result of this incident Murphy suspended his tour and accused his opponents of orchestrating mobs to intimidate him, stating 'The blame lies at the door of Yes Scotland. They should stop this intimidation.' On 16 September the *Independent* ran a headline claiming that Scotland was 'A nation divided against itself.' The evidence? Swearing, heckling, and a claim by George Galloway that a member of the public said he would 'face a bullet.'[85] As Iain Macwhirter points out in *Disunited Kingdom*, a wider narrative about thuggery developed, 'largely on the basis of Rowling and the Murphy stories, the 2014 referendum campaign was widely reported as bitter and divisive because of the brutal and undemocratic tactics of the "cybernats" and other Yes supporters.'[86] The story of trolls targeting JK Rowling had rumbled on for some time after the best-selling author highlighted tweets that had been sent to her when she spoke out in favour of union. Perhaps most worryingly of all, even after the Scottish Police Federation's two calls for calm on the issue, the narrative of hostility, bullying and divisiveness became so prevalent that confirmation bias served to conflate the Federation's remarks with a dark and negative image of political activity leading up to the poll, 'even this warning became part of the ongoing story of street violence and intimidation and was tendentiously reported as a warning about violence to both sides of the campaign,' notes Macwhirter.[87]

The surge in increasingly frenetic coverage was of course the product of panic setting in after the unforeseen 7 September poll (a poll on 4 September, in contrast, published by the *Herald*, put support for Yes at just 25%).[88] A look at the front page headlines in UK newspapers between 1-17 September is therefore revealing. Excluding the *Scotsman* and the *Herald*, there were only two front page stories referring to independence prior to 7 September and the fateful poll: 'Yes vote could cause Sterling crash' (*Telegraph*) and 'Scottish universities fear science brain drain' (*Guardian*). A dramatic shift in the prominence of coverage can be seen across the front pages on the 7 September: all are negative or alarmist including, 'Scotland: the independence crisis' (*Independent*), 'Miliband: we'll put guards on Scottish border' (*Mail*), 'Yes leads in Scots poll shock' (*Sunday Times*). On Monday 8 September 2014 The *Daily Telegraph* proclaimed there were 'Ten days to save Britain,' while front page headlines in other newspapers were also of that order: 'Last stand to keep the union' (*Guardian*), 'Ten days to save the United Kingdom' (*Independent*), 'Parties unite in last-ditch bid to save the union' (*Times*), 'Don't let me be last Queen of Scotland' (*Mirror*), 'Queen's fear over break up of Britain' (*Mail*), while the *Sun*, never prepared to be outdone, ran with, 'Scots vote chaos: jocky horror show.' The following days would see variations on these themes appear regularly on front pages: 'Don't rip apart our family' (*Mail*), 'Mortgage risk if Scots vote Yes' (*Guardian*), 'Fear and loathing in the battle for Scotland' (*Independent*), 'Financial turmoil hits Scotland' (*Times*), 'Seriously Nasty Party' (*Mail*), 'A nation divided against itself' (*Independent*) and 'Money floods out of UK "over Yes vote fears"' (*Telegraph*).

The uniformity of themes present across the British press in this crucial timeframe was arguably offset by widely available alternative viewpoints online and, to lesser extent, on broadcast media. However, the pervasiveness of front pages, both in framing time and in embedding broad narratives, remains profoundly significant. Whatever is printed in black and white on the front of UK titles will almost certainly be discussed on social and broadcast media, and, indeed, will shape the stories that end up in news bulletins. Newspapers such as the *Mail* maintain a level of influence on BBC coverage that Robert Peston and others have lamented.[89] On top of that there is the prominent and pervasive physical presence of front page headlines. As David Patrick reflected during the referendum, 'it remains the case that an individual walking past a newsstand in the period analysed would be presented to a pro-union headline almost half the time.'[90] The physical presence of newspapers and the continuing visual impact of their front pages means that, whether consumers buy them or not, their influence is inescapable.

Conclusion

Alan Cochrane, the *Telegraph's* Scottish Editor, refers in his campaign memoir to a request from the head of the Better Together campaign, Alistair Darling, to spike an unflattering column, 'It's not really good journalism but what the hell does journalism matter? This is much more important.'[91] Cochrane was inadvertently flagging up the underlying democratic problem that was to prove so deleterious to the Scottish media establishment: on the one hand a depletion of journalism's credibility across the board, on the other, a sense that loyalty to the status quo trumped all other concerns. That there was a level of complicity between certain journalists and the campaign to keep Scotland in the union is perhaps unsurprising. The nature of the question could hardly have been of greater political import: impacting on individual identities and calling upon deep ideological and constitutional loyalties. What is more surprising is the lack of self-awareness among the press pack in Scotland as to how narrow the role of Scottish journalism had become. It was far too cosy in its own consensus and far too wiling to dismiss the massive process taking place outside. A small, but telling example, was a comic gesture at the Liberal Democrats 2014 party conference in the form of a note (accompanied by a gift of Tunnocks caramel wafers) thanking journalists because, amongst other feats, they had 'helped save the union'.[92] Had the note referred to the press's assistance in an election victory, it would certainly have provoked far greater attention. But on certain issues such as independence, the political and media establishment are capable of forming a cast iron consensus, particularly if there is a perceived threat to the established order. Avowedly pro-independence journalist Jamie Maxwell sees the issue of bias as a symptom of the 'establishment instincts' prevalent in much of the UK press, 'Most of the print press wasn't even trying to disguise its bias … it upset their sense of metropolitan decency - and, on a much more basic level, their very British commitment to reform through parliamentary channels.'

The media's affinity with the British establishment and its cadet branch in Scotland is, as we've discussed, partly to do with the nature of journalism in an increasingly unequal, socially stratified, UK. As Yes Scotland's Head of Digital, Stewart Kirkpatrick, pointed out, extreme though much of the coverage was, 'There was nothing wrong with the scrutiny that the Yes side was put under during the independence referendum, what was lacking was the No side being put under the same kind of scrutiny.' The case for Britain did not have to be made: it was often assumed to be self-evident. The threat to the fabric of society, 'the other' was never considered to be the anti-social habits of the British ruling classes, still less their highly questionable record on specific issues like the economy or defence. Alongside the hard economic threat prevalent in much of the coverage was an equally virulent appeal to identity. In perhaps the most nationalistic headline printed by any newspaper in recent years, the *Daily Telegraph's* 'Our soldiers lost their lives trying to preserve the UK. What will their families say?' from 13 September was probably the pinnacle of press hysteria. It was, quite literally, a blood and soil appeal to British identity. In this sense, the great irony about the British media's fraught coverage of the referendum was its own nationalism. Not the civic, reformist nationalism prevalent amongst the Yes movement, but rather, its own tendency for what Michael Billig describes as 'banal nationalism'. Billig has studied the UK media and has observed the manner in which the press in particular tends to frame news in terms of national identity, 'All the papers, whether tabloid or quality, and whether left or right-wing, address their readers as members of the nation.'[93]

As can be seen in coverage of controversial issues that are seen to pose a threat to the integrity of Britain, such as immigration, or terrorism for example, the press subtly differentiates between its 'national' readership and the 'other'. Lacking self-awareness, or the capacity to frame multiple identities, 'The newspaper addresses 'us', its readers, as if 'we' are all nationals of the same state: it tells 'us' of 'home' news,' writes Billig. The essential problem that was thrown open, when this banal nationalism was exposed last year, is that in creating a unifying 'us' there must also be a corresponding 'them'. That the latter group turned out to be 1.6 million Scots who also happen to remain citizens of the United Kingdom outlines the scale of this rupture.

Yet the democratic case for a Scottish media is not about simply replacing one banal nationalism with another. Rather, it's about seeking a better media landscape that can incorporate and express different identities and a range of political beliefs and social backgrounds: beyond that of an inherently conservative 'middle Scotland'. It is also about having media spaces that can speak to the whole nation, with all its multiple identities, in a manner that is rational, respectful and accessible to all. The solution to the hysteria of the UK press is better journalism, not the formation of partisan media. When Richard Walker gave the *Sunday Herald*'s endorsement to Yes, his reasoning was simple, 'Scotland's media should reflect the diversity of opinion within the country. We believe that in a real democracy the public should have access to a wide range of views and opinions. The media should not speak with one voice.'[94] If Scotland is to be the kind of diverse, modern, democratic society that many imagined it might become through independence, it will need to found a better media to give voice to the many identities, loyalties and passions that it contains. Not least to ensure that they can, at least on a good day, talk to each other.

3

British Broadcasting

The media do not transmit an idea which happens to
have been fed into them. It matters precious little what
has been fed into them: it is the media themselves, the
pervasiveness and importance of abstract, centralised,
standardised, one to many communication, which itself
automatically engenders the core idea of nationalism.

Ernest Gellner, *Nations and Nationalism* [95]

The refinement of broadcasting technology in the early twentieth-century was accompanied by widespread concerns about the capacity of the medium to do ill if it fell into the wrong hands. In part, this was because early radio (much like the internet a century later) was at first the domain of amateur enthusiasts, revelling in a new tech hobby. In its earliest incarnations the 'wireless' was thought of as a technology that would come to replace the telephone: the concept of broadcasting as a service for mass audiences to engage in passively, for a small number at the centre to speak to the many, was not perceived at first.[96] This is why the licence fee actually predates the formation of the BBC by around 20 years: it was the product of anxiety about the radical new powers that 'wireless telegraphy' offered.

The BBC's first Director General, son of the manse Lord John Reith, commenced his great elevating mission: to inform, educate and entertain at a time when the British Empire was at its greatest extent. This was also the era, just after the monumental carnage of the Great War, in which the British state was expanding, a process that would later be completed with the central planning necessitated by World War Two and post-war nationalisation. This formative period would have a profound influence on the character of the BBC that can still be discerned today. As the *Economist* has argued, 'Many European countries, traumatised by defeat or collaboration, remade their states from first principles, often pushing power away from the tainted centre. In Britain, victory sanctified and strengthened Westminster and Whitehall.' Part of this legacy involves unprecedented levels of central control (Britain is still more centralised than any OECD country other than New Zealand).[97] It was perhaps inevitable that the BBC would develop a mission focused on broadcasting news from the centre to the provinces, and for that matter, the imperial colonies and dominions. An obvious point of contrast was post-war West Germany, where broadcasting was left on Allied orders to the regional Land governments. Paul Hodkinson has emphasised the particular importance of broadcasting to the UK:

> Especially in countries such as the UK, where prominent content was often broadcast simultaneously to the whole country, it became possible for the entire nation to sit down 'together', digesting the same stories, ideas or music at the same time. This had profound implications for citizens' everyday mutual awareness of one another and the distinct national culture that they formed.[98]

In this sense Britain, as a centralised twentieth-century nation, was constructed on the airwaves. This led to notions in the UK and beyond of a greater sense of national unity. As US President Herbert Hoover remarked, radio was 'revolutionizing the political debates that underlie political action under our principles of Government… It physically makes us literally one people on all occasions of general public interest.'[99] Several key historic moments of the era: the abdication of Edward VIII in 1936 (featuring a live broadcast introduced by Reith himself) and later the televised Coronation, added to a sense of common national experience. Just as print had facilitated the development of the 'imagined community', so broadcasting technology deepened the sense of Britain as a unitary state with one audience. *British* broadcasting reified the nation state and its definitive continuity, at a time of flux and change. The role of broadcasting in constructing the modern nation state may be particularly significant in Britain, where broadcasting has often acted as a bridge to promote continuity with the past. As David Cannadine argues, the British monarchy in particular has benefited, 'coverage of the great ceremonials,' says Cannadine, 'has enhanced the picture of grandeur and fairytale splendour which Reith and BBC Radio did so much to promote.'[100]

In a country like the UK, with a highly contested 'national' culture, institutions take on an aggrandised, almost sacred, role. They serve an awkward and very British task that encompasses everything from the mundane day-to-day functions of dusty bureaucracy, to acting as precious vessels for national identity. We think of the BBC and NHS as fair and virtuous, because Britain needs them to be. Of course these institutions, like so many others at the heart of Britain, are all reaching a tipping point. Their reserves of social and economic capital are depleted: increasingly their defence has to revert to broad abstract statements of principle. Yet without them, there is little else for the realm to fall back on. They were created in the image of a postwar, social democratic Britain that is now nearing extinction. Both were too iconic to be privatised after the new Thatcherite consensus was established, so were instead required to adopt internal markets: to contract-in the services, the jargon and the ethos of private enterprise.

Despite the globalisation of certain aspects of the media (in particular ownership), the production of newspapers, television programmes and news is often persistently reliant on familiarity with a given territory. This is not only about the inevitable need for a measure of 'local knowledge' but also about a more complex need to maintain the link and indeed the identity, of a certain area. At a UK level, despite the generational shifts that devolution has brought about, broadcast media remains stubbornly centralised. Public service broadcasting and the strength of the BBC model in terms of longevity and overall popularity is deeply embedded in the British psyche. The media regulator OFCOM defines public service broadcasting in a manner that is strikingly similar to the rhetoric of Lord Reith:

> To reflect and strengthen our cultural identity, through high-quality UK national and regional programming;
>
> To support a tolerant and inclusive society, through the availability of programmes which reflect the lives of different people and communities within the UK, encourage a better understanding of different cultures and perspectives and, on occasion, bring the nation together for shared experiences.[101]

The final clause was perhaps most thoroughly demonstrated by the coverage of the London Olympics in 2012: an event that was explicitly pitched as a celebration of Britishness (it would later be cited as a reference point in David Cameron's effort to 'beat back' Scottish independence).[102] The BBC, one of several key institutions that hold together the British nation state, was at the heart of this display of unity, greatness and continuity. In fact its dual role is even deeper than that. As Tony Ageh (the Controller of BBC Internet who introduced the iPlayer) points out 'if the BBC were a bank it wouldn't be Barclays or HSBC. It would be the Bank of England. It sits to one side of those that compete for business and safeguards the entire system itself for the benefit of all – providers and public alike.' Yet the BBC has shown itself to be incapable of standing aloof from the scandals that have rocked the British establishment over the past decade. Accusations of mishandling during the referendum was just one example of a whole list of scandals and allegations the corporation has had to face down in recent years. In part, this is the lot of any large bureaucratic organisation far more vulnerable and exposed to criticism in a networked age, but this should not make us lose sight of how rapid the erosion of that status has taken place. In 2005 Tessa Jowell proclaimed 'The BBC is as much a part of British life as the NHS.' She did so off the back of a vast public consultation about the national broadcaster. 75% of some 30,000 responses were positive, with 'high quality news programmes' amongst the top three factors cited.[103] In this sense the BBC's current 'battle' for its existence is telling. The BBC, with its universal ethos, is one of a small number of institutions that serve as the glue holding Britain together. Charlotte Higgins explained the coming showdown in the *Guardian* in July 2015:

> The BBC is still clinging fiercely to the Reithian principle that the corporation exists to do more than to plug the gaps left by commercial broadcasters – that it creates the invisible but strong filaments of shared national memory, emotion and experience that bind every inhabitant of these islands together. That is the vision that the BBC would like to sustain. That is the vision that gives it philosophical licence to provide something for everyone, from 1Xtra to Wolf Hall, and the means and heft to ensure it can.[104]

The notion of a BBC making programmes for all, complementing its basic task of keeping the airwaves public, is under threat thanks to the arrival of Culture Secretary John Wittingdale. Already it has had to accept an unprecedented effort by government to effectively slash its income by almost a fifth (by making it pay for providing free TV licences to over 75s). The vision that has been presented in the government's Green Paper is of a far smaller BBC which leaves popular programming to the commercial sector and focuses on areas that tend to have less commercial viability such as news and current affairs.[105] Rather than looking across the board at public service broadcasting, with its massive cultural remit, the emphasis seems to be on preventing the BBC duplicating products that are available to consumers on other channels. Its idealised vision of the corporation, it seems, is more akin to PBS in the United States: low-budget, esoteric, educational. As Higgins reminds us, the coming years will be definitive for the future of the Beeb and with it the entire notion of Britain ever again becoming a social democratic country. 'In the end,' she concludes, 'these are questions that cut to the heart of what British society consists of, and what kind of nation we want to be ... Britain will have the BBC it deserves.'

Out of this comes a complex set of political questions about Scotland's place in all of it. Frequently left unexamined, largely due to the immensely centralised nature of British public life, working out what impact charter renewal will have on Scotland is far from straightforward. While the presence of 56 SNP MPs in the House of Commons ought to give Scottish priorities more voice in the process, and while the BBC acknowledged in its 2014-15 annual report that it needed to respond to changes in Scotland post-referendum, there are few precedents to suggest a radically different settlement for Scotland would emerge.[106] A common thread in terms of broadcasting policy in the UK is an extreme reluctance, whatever the ascendant politics of the day, to offer Scotland greater control over its broadcasting. What is most concerning about this is not so much the privileging of metropolitan media (large scale media operations always have an incentive to centralise structures) but rather the fact that anxiety about the capacity of Scotland to deliver the goods has often been shared by the natives too. As Maggie Sweeney points out:

> Examination of the long interaction between London and Scotland over the years clearly reveals the extent of the reluctance on London's part to confer greater autonomy on Scotland within both the BBC and the commercial sector - the constant fear being that there would be an inevitable dilution in the quality and scope of output. And it has to be said that similar anxieties continue to be expressed from time to time north of the border too. [107]

Sweeney's observation is a significant one: insecurity about Scotland's ability to populate the airwaves is part London-centrism and part Scottish cringe. Sitting awkwardly between a national culture and a regional policy, its management has often, though not always, been conservative and provincial in outlook meaning that Scottish broadcasting has often been plagued by its 'novel' role. With very little to incentivise innovation, current structures have created broadcast media north of the border that is simply not fit for purpose.

The BBC, still by far the biggest player in Scotland's media ecology, remains stubbornly attached to maintaining power in London. This, far more than the behaviour of any single journalist, editor or producer, was crucial to the controversial outcomes of the corporation's referendum coverage. Some mistakes were glaring, some vital developments were glossed over, but the far greater issue that emerged was about the underlying structural problems that the BBC faces: a struggle to speak to diverse audiences in these isles and to adapt to rapid constitutional developments. Much of the outcry provoked and many of the accusations of bias from both sides in the referendum campaign were rooted in these deeply embedded issues. The corporation's approach to the hinterland beyond the M25 is defined by its 'nations and regions' policy, that some see as little more than a fig-leaf masking a London-centric culture. As Neil Blain and David Hutchison put it:

> The 'nations' and 'regions' tactic ('nations and regions means 'not London') is a response from institutions reluctant to devolve real power, which construct this offering as a means to retain control in London. 'Nations and Regions' proponents (including the regulator Ofcom) have traditionally been uncomfortable about real divergence across the UK. Regional cooking, local wildlife and folk culture are welcome as constituting difference, but ideological and political difference unnerve the ambassadors of the nations and regions policy.[108]

As mentioned above, the claim that there is not a Scottish media, does not claim that there is no *media in Scotland*, but rather, for obvious structural and political reasons, the development of a modern media in Scotland is self-evidently subordinate within the wider structures that control it, in this case the BBC network. This plays a crucial role in how talent is developed and careers shaped. When journalist and broadcaster Lesley Riddoch made her plans to return to Scotland clear to superiors in London as a trainee, the response was revealing:

> It was thought to be outrageously and wastefully unusual. I was on the BBC's news training scheme, there was eight people out of two thousand applicants a year and so I finished that in London, had done attachments all over the place, and quite evidently the next path for people from

> there was to become cannon fodder in the newsrooms, the
> TV and radio newsrooms in London, until they were farmed
> out to be correspondents ... So when I said I was going back
> to Scotland there was absolute horror and the guy running
> the course actually said to me, "you would not have got
> on this course if we thought you had such low ambitions."

As the divisive 'parachuting in' of network journalists to cover the closing stages of the Scottish referendum story in 2014 reminds us, there is little tangible evidence to suggest that such attitudes have changed over the years. The most obvious reason for this provincial approach is the fact that BBC Scotland simply lacks the clout or resources to function as a national broadcaster, even though it is often called upon to fulfil that role.

The Audience Question

In October 2010 David Dimbleby, presenting an episode of *Question Time* from Glasgow, inadvertently dramatised the BBC's struggle to represent diverse audiences throughout the UK. Dimbleby repeatedly cut off then Deputy First Minister Nicola Sturgeon when her responses referred to Scottish rather than 'UK-wide' issues, because the programme was for a 'UK audience'. Most of the episode, despite being broadcast from north of the border, was devoted to a government reduction in housing benefit and focused on the cost of housing in London.[109] Similar instances have occurred on the *Daily Politics* and other current affairs shows: often the need to have a Scottish commentator or politician appearing remotely while guests in the south appear in the studio, makes the divide even more acute. This confusion about who ought to be speaking to what audience from where reigned supreme during the final days of the referendum campaign, but it has been an issue that the BBC has struggled to grapple with for some time.

In part this problem is a creation of the lopsided nature of the UK's current constitutional settlement: 'national' UK issues decided and debated at Westminster are often, in fact, English-only but are nonetheless presented as headlines in pan-UK news bulletins. Lecturer and former BBC broadcast journalist Ewan Crawford, is clear about where the root of such problems lie:

> The BBC far too often pretends that its audience is uniform. Clearly that isn't the case and it defaults too often within the current structure, which is logical from their point of view. If you have 85% of the population in England and your news and current affairs programming is going out across the whole of the UK, then clearly from a programme maker's point of view, you want to interest the majority of your audience. My issue is when you have such a divergent policy and political environment ... between Scotland and England... there has to be a change in that structure, because effectively when David Dimbleby made his comment ... in effect he was privileging one audience over another.

Unease at this curious position has led to a kind of institutional paralysis within BBC Scotland, one that was always waiting to be exposed when Scottish politics heated up in the wake of the SNP's victories over Labour. The fiery political passions invoked on both sides of the constitutional debate made this fundamental question more explicit. While the BBC is used to being attacked from both sides when it covers controversial political events, its institutional set up in Scotland was essentially incapable of properly addressing concerns raised about quality and impartiality. The BBC's Scotland Correspondent James Cook pointed out the extent to which both sides were adamant that coverage was biased one way or the other, 'We came under an incredible amount of pressure. I think there are people very high up in the Labour party, in fact I know there are, who still sincerely believe that the output from Pacific Quay was outrageously biased in favour of the Yes campaign and the SNP.' The most obvious example of this mentality was an astonishing outburst from Labour MP Ian Davidson who branded *Newsnight Scotland* 'Newsnat' Scotland live on air and accused personnel working on the programme, including presenter Isabel Fraser, of actively favouring a pro-nationalist agenda, stating:

> I've already complained, as has the Labour Party on a number of occasions about the way in which Newsnat Scotland behaves and I think you are clearly biased and have been for some time against the unionist parties, and if that causes you concern that you've just got to recognise that politics is about people exchanging views and you're not above the fray and if you want to stand for election, do so. Otherwise try and be more neutral.[110]

The National Question

Concern within the BBC about its relationship with Scottish nationalism goes back to the 1920s. The removal of the corporation's first Scottish Regional Director, David Cleghorn Thomson in 1932 was partly related to his perceived nationalist sympathies. After his removal, according to George McKechnie:

> The BBC's fear of nationalism even extended to issuing instructions to a London executive to investigate feelings of nationalism among the staff; and in the wake of the sacking of Thomson to carry out soundings across the Scottish establishment to confirm that they were now

assured that the BBC and its executives in Scotland were
not sympathetic to Scottish nationalism.[111]

It is therefore unsurprising that shrill complaints from across
the political spectrum about the BBC's coverage of nationalism
have been a regular feature of Scottish politics ever since the SNP
began to make electoral gains in the 1960s. Alasdair Milne's 1968
documentary, *Where do we go from here?* about the fallout from the
Winnie Ewing's landmark by-election victory in Hamilton, is a
case in point. Milne, who would later become Director General of
the BBC, recalled in his autobiography:

> Two hours before transmission, I had a phone call from Tam
> Dayell, younger then but no less radical in his views, who
> warned me that if we went ahead with the programme
> "the effect would be more drastic than Hiroshima". We did
> go ahead and the building stood...Both parties [Labour
> and Conservative] clearly believed there was a strong SNP
> cell in Queen Margaret Drive.[112]

The documentary, among the BBC's first attempts at substantive
engagement with the national question, was in fact well received
by the public, if not by the ranks of the Labour MPs in Scotland, as
former BBC executive Pat Walker recalled:

> The programme attracted a huge Scottish audience and
> also a great deal of criticism especially from Scottish MPs
> who complained that it was ill-balanced and misleading.
> But there were just as many people ready with praise,
> including the BCS [Broadcasting Council for Scotland]
> where the general opinion was that it was time politicians
> realised there was a mood abroad in the country.[113]

At a UK level, it is worth remembering that the BBC's recent institutional history involved a period of extreme turbulence just as the national question was becoming acute in Scotland. Milne's resignation, forced by a new Thatcherite Chairman of the BBC Governors in 1987, was a watershed moment for a BBC that in the 1970s and 80s had to struggle with a vast array of challenges it had never before had to confront. Jean Seaton, the Official Historian of the BBC, sees the Thatcher era as, 'a tumultuous time of uncomfortable, relentless overturning of expectations and ways of life, which tested the BBC severely.' As a result, 'by the late eighties the BBC was all too often the story, vulnerable to new commercial and political models, its capacity to exercise political balance tested by three great Conservative election victories, an unelectable opposition, and the emergence of a new third party.'[114] If there is more than an echo of familiarity with the current political tensions, it is because the BBC has always struggled in the face of radical political shifts. The years leading up to the 1979 referendum are a case in point.

When Alistair Hetherington became controller of BBC Scotland (after winning renown over the course of two decades as editor of the *Guardian*) his attempts to gain greater autonomy from London were met with bureaucratic intransigence. Remarkably for such a respected figure, Hetherington's stint as controller lasted only three years, before he was removed and demoted to a role managing BBC Radio Highland. Like many other careers in the media that have moved northwards, his was a seemingly needless journey into undeserved obscurity. The reasons for this debacle are, however, fairly transparent. Hetherington's term was not a happy one because he sought to make headway on the then highly topical issue of how the corporation should respond to the prospect of a devolved Scottish Assembly. Influenced by assurances from Labour Secretary of State for Scotland, Willie Ross, that broadcasting would be amongst the powers devolved to the new body, he seemed genuinely optimistic that a rational case for expanding BBC Scotland's remit would meet with approval from his superiors.[115] Yet in doing so, the new controller ran up against multiple obstacles, even though his demands for 'mini devolution', as he would later describe it, were far from radical. 'In essence it said that we must be prepared for a Scottish Assembly, that BBC Scotland must have more freedom to decide for itself the way its money was used, and that its first priority must be that of strengthening news and current affairs,' this was Hetherington's self-described mission.[116]

For former *Reporting Scotland* presenter Kenneth Roy, 'these symbolic events introduced a note of high drama, even personal tragedy, into the plodding long-running whodunnit known as public service broadcasting north of the border.' The struggle to wrest a measure of control (London's writ was so total that, as Roy points out, even an extra key for an unmanned studio in Dundee could not be ordered without permission from authorities in the capital) was an indication of how the BBC would struggle to cope with the increasing significance of constitutional politics in Scotland. It was such a mindset that Hetherington sought to challenge but, as Roy recalls, 'when he asked for more money, more network exposure for Scottish programmes and more autonomy, he was confronted instead with a demand to notify 58 bureaucrats in the south before he was allowed to spend £800 on new titles for a programme.'[117]

A great deal has changed at BBC Scotland in the intervening decades, though the need to go through a bureaucratic hierarchy remains suffocating: in July 2014 staff at Pacific Quay expressed frustration that they had to phone an outsourced company in the West Midlands for permission to open and close window blinds and remove partitions.[118] Roy notes that up until Hetherington's arrival the consensus in the north had been to adopt a risk averse approach, 'In this narrow ambition to mind its own back, the BBC in Scotland succeeded all too well.'

This is not to suggest that there was not progress in the final decades of the last century on certain fronts. BBC Scotland's Head of Drama Pharic Maclaren achieved legendary status during this period, particularly with an adaptation of Lewis Grassic Gibbon's *Sunset Song*, premised on the notion that 'Scotland must break into the network on a regular basis.'[119] However, the most significant development was the launch of BBC Radio Scotland in November 1978. Initially the new arrival did not meet with universal praise. Neal Ascherson described it thus, 'Radio Kailyard or Back Green Calling is what Hugh MacDiarmid at his deadliest called an ugly beast without wings: a speckled hen whose horizon goes no further than the end of the little minister's glebe.'[120] As Scottish society began face down the massive existential challenges presented by the 1980s, BBC Scotland began to find a voice for itself, was instrumental in rattling the British establishment during the 1987 Zircon affair and its output began to chime with the voice of 'civic Scotland'. Mrs Thatcher's notorious 'we in Scotland' interview was a definitive moment of drama in a decade laden with political theatre played out across the Scottish media.

Expansion

Where Hetherington's tenure as controller was fraught and unfulfilled, that of his longest serving successor John McCormick, who ran BBC Scotland from 1992 to 2004, was more fruitful: with turnover increasing from £60 million to £170 million. Remarkably, for such a public role, critics of McCormick's controllership are hard to find, a *Herald* profile on his retirement was glowing:

> During his term of office, a dramatically successful revolution has taken place within BBC Scotland. Under his quiet, steady leadership, the organisation has doubled its

local programming and network contributions, and seen its workforce increase significantly. If there is one word to describe his contribution to Scottish broadcasting, it's 'quality'. [121]

Behind the figures, numerous smaller developments had created a broadcaster in Scotland with greater gravitas and reach. 1992, for example, saw BBC Scotland's first live coverage of election night results. Tellingly, the case for this was made on the basis of different results in Scotland (Tory losses) being glossed over by the network in the 1987 contest.[122] This was also the era of the 'Scottishification' of many aspects of public life, newly confident Scottish accents and brands could be seen and heard across a range of fields, from pop music to the private sector. Part of McCormick's success can be attributed to the emphasis that he placed on the news and current affairs side of the operation: a common understanding that journalism was at the heart of BBC Scotland's offering was freely extoled. 'The core of BBC Scotland's output has always been journalism … John McCormick would tell the staff that in the newsroom: whatever else we do, it's all important, but the core audience comes to BBC Scotland for journalism, news and current affairs. That's what drives the audience,' says Derek Bateman, who presented *Good Morning Scotland* from 1996 to 2006. On one level both internal and external controversies about the performance of BBC Scotland have always related to how it defines its priorities: something that is inherently more complicated than in other parts of the corporation. BBC Radio Scotland in particular, though limited to one channel (albeit with occasional medium wave opt outs) is expected to perform multiple roles: to offer a schedule that is part Radio 2, part Radio 4, part Five Live. Yes the focus generated by foregrounding news and current affairs can perhaps be credited with generating an *esprit de corps* now almost entirely lacking at Pacific Quay.

The station's news and current affairs output was award winning and far more expansive and open than it is today. There was a monthly Scottish opt-out of *Question Time*, a substantially better resourced *Good Morning Scotland*, while offerings like the *Lesley Riddoch Programme* regularly toured the country, seeking out new stories and alternative angles on the day's headlines. The programme's Editor, Alison Balharry, recalls the breadth of their remit, facilitated in no small part by a camper van kitted out for outside broadcast:

> I can remember we went to Denmark in 2000 to cover their second in/out vote on the EMU. We broadcast from bang in the middle of Copenhagen's central City Hall Square. It was a fantastic resource ... we had the staffing levels, and experience, that allowed us to be ambitious. Of course we regularly toured around Scotland, it took the programme out of the studio to communities... living, breathing, learning what was happening in the country. I don't believe the news factory, one size fits all, approach works, it has to be about engaging directly with the audience in a meaningful, not tokenistic way. That needs to be properly resourced across BBC sites in Scotland, as well as at Pacific Quay in Glasgow.

In addition to this broad minded approach to coverage, the reputation for quality and emphasis on current affairs allowed Radio Scotland to compete with the best output in the UK. *Good Morning Scotland* became a runner up to *Today* at the Sony Awards, a remarkable achievement given that the former has always operated with a much smaller budget, while BBC Radio Scotland would go on to win the title of Station of the Year.[123] Derek Bateman recalls the prospect of first taking on the role of fronting *Good Morning Scotland*, 'it was a massive moment. I was terrified all week, because it really meant something … it was a really serious programme and you had to be bloody good to do it and when you weren't people told you.'

Within radio output, the more recent move away from current affairs coverage in favour of phone-in shows and music has been attributed to Head of Radio Jeff Zycinski, who has overseen this shift. 'Ahead of the referendum campaign, in managerial terms' says Balharry 'you had a head of news whose main focus was on television output, and a head of radio whose main focus was on topical and features programming, radio news lacked a champion, and, I'd say, suffered disproportionately in resource terms, as a result, when it came to the front loaded cuts.'

An announcement of changes to put political coverage 'at the core' of BBC Radio Scotland after the referendum from Zycinski, amounted to very little material change. In reality this 'commitment' consisted of rebranding *Morning Call*, presented by Kaye Adams, to the *Kaye Adams Programme* (while re-categorising it as topical programming) extending *Newsdrive* by 30 minutes, and adding a new satirical panel show to the schedule.[124]

More With Less

One of the most difficult challenges in understanding media is that of remembering that behind every presenter, journalist or individual personality, there is a dedicated team working to deliver a quality media product. At BBC Scotland, the façade – what viewers see on their screen and hear on their radio – may not have changed in any dramatic or instantly discernible way. Instead, the station's malaise has been a steady dripping away of resources and staff, along with a sense of collective purpose and morale. The symptoms are not, therefore, obvious to the untrained eye. Bateman, whose reputation for candour belies the fact that many of his views on the BBC are shared with colleagues still within the organisation, believes that the difference in quality is obvious, as are the reasons behind it:

> Resources and talent. That's was missing in the media today ... to me that is the key: if you've got good journalists and you've got resources, and, at that time, we did ... You had well trained producers who knew what the programmes were for, you had things like departmental editors so that there was an editor for all of the weekend output, as opposed to the daily output. So that was someone who took pride in every programme under his tutelage ... at the moment there's one editor who covers all radio news and sport, now that's a meaningless job, because you can't do that. We had, not just producers for every edition of *GMS*, you had a daily editor ... Now they have two or three people scrabbling together every programme, it's difficult to take pride in what you're producing, you know that the management don't care, they give you that very clear message. And I think that eventually bleeds through, it shows, it shows on air.

According to such accounts, it is neglect, not conspiracy, that is the source of the BBC's trouble in Scotland. On McCormick's retirement in 2004 the task of fighting Scotland's corner fell to current director, Ken MacQuarrie. MacQuarrie's most notable achievement has been the establishment of a dedicated Gaelic language channel, BBC Alba, perhaps always destined to be overshadowed by the unenviable task of taking an axe to resources and staff numbers across the board. MacQuarrie's tenure had barely begun before he was tasked with implementing 25% savings as part of a network-wide drive.[125] This led to the departure of BBC Scotland's then head of News and Current Affairs, Blair Jenkins. Jenkins explains the cause of his resignation:

I knew there were programmes that I was responsible for
that were thinly resourced at that time. The notion that
you could make 25% cuts without damaging the quality
of the output I felt was just completely wrong and it was
just the wrong time to be doing it with everything that
was happening in Scotland. In 2006 of course no one knew
that we were a year away from the first SNP government
being elected, but you could tell in Scotland that there was
a lot going on and there was a national debate ... It wasn't
the time to be scaling back on your journalistic coverage.

The events surrounding the departure of Jenkins can be seen as
illustrative of an ongoing set of problems. While its status and
funding continues to be eroded, the pace of events in Scotland has
increased significantly and public demands for a broader range
of coverage, particularly in terms of news and current affairs,
have never been louder. In 2011 a further round of savings was
announced meaning that 120 jobs, 1 in 10 of the BBC's workforce
in Scotland, would be lost due to the freezing of the licence fee
by the new coalition government. Management at BBC Scotland
has frequently been criticised for the way it has handled the cuts,
particularly in its attempts to scale back even further in the direct
run up to the referendum. NUJ Scotland organiser Paul Holleran
describes his union's strong opposition to such a move:

Of all the things that bad management could do, or a decision that could be taken, one of the worst that I've ever
come across in all the years that I've been a union official,
or as a journalist, was that decision by BBC Scotland ... they
introduced 17% worth of cuts up front, before 2014 kicked
in. You had the Commonwealth Games coming up, you had
the Ryder Cup, you had the commemoration of the start
of World War One and you had the biggest political story,

probably in history of modern journalism and they made a massive amount of cuts right across the newsrooms … They didn't need to, those cuts are now taking place in England and Wales and Northern Ireland in 2015, but they decided they were going to do it then.

In the short term the effects of this may have been mitigated by the setting up of a referendum unit with an additional £5 million for coverage, in effect partially restoring some of the budget that had been lost. Although this too proved controversial, given the emphasis placed on bringing up James Naughtie to present *Good Morning Scotland* two days a week. Holleran also claims that staffing numbers within the unit were opaque while many of the new temporary journalistic posts created were filled by 15 trainees. 'We'd been told there'd be 50 new members of staff, we saw about 15 trainees, who were all very good … but nowhere near the scale that they promised.' The core issue in all these instances was about whether the country needs and is prepared to fund well-resourced broadcast journalism of its own, in order to cover big stories on the horizon. Jenkins remains adamant that the question of resources is key:

> I felt it was unacceptable to be cutting back on the funding of journalism in Scotland at that time and I think events have confirmed me in that view. There are still a number of very good people who work at BBC Scotland but I know the struggle with resources. People I'm still in touch with tell me how much they struggle with lack of resources and I think that's been a large part of the problem, not the entire problem.

As money has haemorrhaged from Pacific Quay, with cuts front loaded and current affairs taking a big hit, the Beeb's status and reputation has, perhaps inevitably, declined as a result. The differ-ence between BBC Scotland before and after such financial shocks is therefore less to do with the attitude or presence of particular journalists or presenters. Rather, it is a toxic combination of declining resources, a decreasing emphasis on quality news and current affairs, and a general failure to respond to wider changes in contemporary Scotland. Of course, part of this can be attrib-uted to issues prevalent in the wider BBC that are too complex to address here. Yet, from whatever angle you look at it, the disparate power relationship between London and Glasgow remains central. In Lesley Riddoch's view, this can be seen very clearly in terms of how commissioning in Scotland has tended to favour comedy and drama in recent years:

> You might think in a BBC world where there's no commer-cials involved ratings don't matter, but they do. So your ratings had to be the same as the BBC average ratings or they would say, why should we be giving more money to a loser network? I'm not a manager but I'm told that was the way it worked. Any of the comedy programmes or enter-tainment programmes would almost inevitably be more expensive than current affairs but they would certainly attract a bigger audience share. And then there's the ques-tion of what kind of current affairs programmes? If you just stick Gordon Brewer in a studio and let him rattle away at two folk who are required to turnout because they're MSPs it may be cheap but it's not exactly riveting TV.

Looked at from this perspective, the fact that innovative program-ming and serious journalism *did* take place during the referendum campaign under the BBC banner, is a credit to the dedication and professionalism of certain journalists. But this cannot distract from the gulf that has developed between staff and management.

Speaking to a Scottish Parliament committee in January 2013 BBC Scotland's Head of News and Current Affairs, John Boothman, downplayed problems with regards to staffing levels:

> As for staffing, BBC Scotland has over the years been very good at multiskilling. Instead of working on individual programmes, people will be working across the output. For example, if you work on "Good Morning Scotland", you will get a break and then work for a lunchtime programme. That model has been tried and tested across the BBC and works for the BBC News channel and a load of other areas.[126]

Boothman's controversial stewardship of his department during the referendum came to an end in June 2015 after a successful bullying complaint was lodged by Zoe MacDonald. The incident made public rumours about low staff morale and confidence in management. The results of an internal staff survey reported by the *Guardian* found that only 19% of news and current affairs staff believed bullying complaints against their managers would have a 'positive outcome', while only 20% felt bullying would be fairly dealt with and a mere 16% had confidence in management decision-making. This was the third staff survey in a row to find staff morale in the Scottish newsroom to be the lowest in the corporation.[127] Whatever the faults of management, there is a far bigger question that needs to be addressed. Namely, how could an organisation, once proud of its well-earned reputation for rigorous journalism, be so extensively called out for its perceived failings by both sides in the referendum? The answers can be found in the deeply unionist and centralised structures that govern the BBC.

Devolution and the *Scottish Six*

In the wake of Scotland's devolution referendum in 1997, a reluctance to cede control of broadcasting to the new Scottish Parliament was accompanied by an almighty furore over whether or not this event ought to herald an opt-out flagship *Scottish Six* news programme. This was a very early demonstration of how poorly such a major shift of democratic control would take into account the crucial role of the media in maintaining a public sphere in Scotland.

According to the writ of the New Labour government of the day, the devolution of political power was expressly not to be accompanied by power over broadcasting. Originally however, there was a big question mark over whether broadcasting would be devolved. For many, the case for doing so was self-evident and democratic. Yet the 2002 autobiography of the Director General who oversaw this period, John Birt, is explicit about how top brass at the corporation worked with politicians to prevent change. Led by Birt, it lobbied senior Labour figures in Westminster to ensure that broadcasting was not devolved. Devolution was viewed as an existential threat by the BBC, which is why it played such a defensive role when faced with what it interpreted as a rise in Scottish nationalism. However, Birt's disdain wasn't just reserved for nationalists. It was more broadly directed at a range of opinion that rallied behind the concept of concrete change in the form a serious Scottish evening bulletin. The former Director General is triumphant about winning the ensuing 'ferocious battle' with colleagues in Scotland over this issue. As Birt explains:

> As devolution loomed as a reality, and the emotional temperature rose, BBC executives in Glasgow, the Broadcasting Council, the Scottish media and even Scottish civil servants all began to support the case for an independent

Six. [...] I resolved to ensure that this potent alliance was not joined by all the main political parties in Scotland in particular the powerful cohort of Scottish Labour politicians.[128]

The Director General's overwhelming disdain for the ceding of autonomy to Scotland goes way beyond institutional conservatism (in other areas he was a controversial moderniser). Rather, this was a remarkably successful attempt by the leader of the BBC to align the organisation with a unionist agenda at the outset of devolution. He would go on to find powerful allies in his campaign against an opt-out news programme:

I wrote to, and then went to see, the new Prime Minister Tony Blair. I expounded not just from the BBC's perspective but from the nation's. I argued that we were one of the few institutions which bound Britain together. BBC news was iconic. Opting out of the *Six* would be a powerful symbol of Scotland moving away from UK-wide institutions. The end of a single, common experience of UK news, would, moreover, encourage separatist tendencies. ... Blair was quick, as ever, to grasp the case. 'Let's fight' he said.[129]

It's worth keeping in mind what Birt and the powerful converts to his agenda were actually fighting. The *Scottish Six* was a modest proposal by any standards. That a country worthy of a parliament was so categorically denied a flagship news programme tells us a great deal about the link between the concentration of media power and the continuity of the state itself. Furthermore, support for the *Six* really was broad based, Donald Dewar was said to be in favour, along with a broad cross party coalition of Scottish opinion, who anticipated the need for such a service to properly hold the Scottish Parliament to account and to situate the politics of a devolved nation within a wider picture. John McCormick was also an advocate of the proposal and later noted his personal chagrin that Birt would take such an approach to the issue: 'To work with politicians to make sure that the *Scottish Six* didn't happen was simply unacceptable. I was surprised and shocked to read that in his book. It depressed me ... I never thought he would do that. You win or lose these arguments on their merits within the BBC. You shouldn't go and drum up political support for your position.'[130]

In response to Birt's refusal Professor Lindsay Paterson of the Broadcasting Council for Scotland branded the episode a 'charade' and expressed dismay at the involvement of New Labour in halting the move. 'The governors have been informed that senior members of the Cabinet oppose an integrated *Scottish Six*,' stated Lindsay, before handing in his resignation.[131] The episode was an example of the inherently inferior place that Scottish priorities occupy within the wider BBC structure. Announcing the corporation's final decision on the *Six*, Baroness Barbara Young explained, 'We felt we had to take the best decision, not just for Scotland, but for the reporting of news in the rest of the UK'. [132]

Ever since that crucial opportunity in 1998 was lost in the face of unionist intransigence, arguments for the development of an authentic and serious Scottish media have fallen on deaf ears. The resultant situation is perverse: serious journalism in Scotland has declined just as the nation embarked on a new democratic adventure. Like proposals for the *Six* before it, the 2008 report of the Scottish Broadcasting Commission, calling for multi-million pound investment in a new public service digital platform, found cross-party support, but was largely ignored when it went south. It is vitally important to place the BBC's controversial coverage of the referendum in this context, given that it was in no small part the result of a systematic neglect of Scottish broadcasting since devolution.

London Arrives

'Just look at the coverage, on any of the channels, suddenly people that have not been part of this debate are flown up to Scotland to give some fake status to things and you have people dotted all over hillsides in Edinburgh doing special reports, and it's this big status thing, oh London's arrived, at last!' Stuart Cosgrove's impassioned complaint summed up the mood within BBC Scotland (on the Beeb's own *John Beattie Programme*) in the final days of the referendum campaign. When the BBC network finally woke up to the significance of the Scottish referendum story at a UK level, it went into panic mode and in doing so exposed the underlying power relationships that govern the corporation. As discussed in Chapter 2, the sudden transformation of the story due to the 'shock' poll of 7 September almost instantaneously altered the news value of what had previously been treated as a political sideshow. The vast news gathering operation of the BBC, with all its international prestige, almost missed the story of the break up of Britain and as a result it panicked.

Paul Holleran, who was in New Broadcasting House the day after the notorious poll broke, describes the scene within the corporation's HQ, 'they were running around like headless chickens ... some of the senior journalists were preparing their backpacks as though they were heading off to Gallipoli to protect the empire. "Come up to keep the natives in line" it was absolutely bizarre...' The sudden appearance of a possible Yes victory on the network's radars created a scramble to give prominence to what could easily have been one of the most totemic news stories of the century. To have missed such a story in their own backyard would have been scandalous for the upper echelons of the BBC. As Cosgrove highlighted, the sudden descent of BBC anchors and news teams in the north showed a disdain for the ability of BBC Scotland to handle a story of such import:

...I've always thought that the idea of BBC Scotland's opt-out capabilities are far too small, far too squeezed and not autonomous enough and therefore as a consequence of that TV that goes out on the network is seen as real telly, and stuff that goes out in Scotland is seen as lesser, less well founded, and somehow of less importance and then when there's big events, what happens is the troops move in....

Unsurprisingly, this improvised response served to create significant resentment within BBC Scotland. After months of research and planning the referendum story, now given international status, was plucked from the control of Pacific Quay by colleagues in the south. According to Alison Balharry, this was the key mistake that the corporation made, by reverting to its centralised instincts at the worst possible moment:

So when it came to the referendum, yes, undoubtedly, mistakes were made from the outset. That was an issue for the whole of the BBC. I don't think BBC Scotland, including Scottish based network correspondents, did anything like as badly as its many critics make out. I think the BBC at a network level, however, was, overall, pretty poor. It appeared to me they treated it like a foreign story, as if they never really got to grips with it. In the final days before the vote individuals, flown up from London based flagship programmes, were still asking why they should even care about the story, declaring they'd be glad when it was over. And of course treating their BBC colleagues in Glasgow like second class citizens. That's what people don't see. There is a hierarchy within the organisation, and not just in geographical terms. The size and current BBC set up, added to relative UK wide audience share, dictates it to an extent. So that structure, if you like, was projected onto the coverage of the referendum.

If there is one way to guarantee alienating a group of journalists, it is to take away a story that they have worked on and to repeat their mistakes. While it remains a single organisation, it is very difficult to perceive such internal differences between the corporation in Glasgow and London. But as we have seen above, disconnect, or a desire for change in Scotland, must always be subordinate to priorities in the south. 'When they saw people coming in and just riding rough-shod over stories that they'd worked on for some time, I think it focused a lot of people's minds, in respect to what the BBC is about, even within the BBC in Scotland,' says Holleran.

Conclusion

On 1 June 2014 protestors gathered outside BBC Scotland's headquarters at Pacific Quay. It was the first of three demonstrations at the site that would take place during the referendum campaign. Growing numbers would attend these events, which were characterised by humour, song, dancing, ropey PA systems and firebrand speeches. Though the topical nature of these protests afforded them significant attention – not least due to attempts to link them to the SNP by prominent BBC figures – there is nothing unprecedented about protest taking place outside BBC premises. In recent years groups have protested against the BBC's coverage of Gaza, its perceived bias in favour of the royal family, child abuse scandals and the portrayal of working class communities. The corporation's coverage of controversial or divisive issues almost inevitably leads to vocal criticism from both sides of any such debate. The difference, as we have seen, is that if one group is represented by the establishment, it will exert its influence via networks of contacts and access. The seeming inability to influence coverage was, for many in the Yes campaign, offset by a newfound sense of agency. This was embodied in an ability to express feeling voiceless against media organisations that they knew maintained a far greater reach than any community or social media campaign could ever hope for. Derec, a freelance designer, interviewed by independent filmmaker Al McMaster at the protest, explained his reasons for attending,

> I first noticed very strong bias I think it was back, I think it was the third or fourth of February 2014 and it was the day that Holyrood passed the same sex marriage bill. It was quite a monumental event, whenever similar legislation was passed in Westminster it got wall to wall coverage, it was number one news item, on every BBC news bulletin, but when it happened at Holyrood the number one news bulletin that day was, I think it was the director of BP or Shell, giving another one of these warnings about independence and how an independent Scotland will not be able to manage its oil.[133]

What such remarks point to is the need for structural change. The limited coverage, the small 'c' conservative parochial outlook, is the product of the systemic failure of the BBC to devolve power in any meaningful way beyond London. BBC Scotland had been made to absorb successive waves of front-loaded cuts, which often had the greatest impact on current affairs output. This served to leave the station chronically under resourced and under staffed, with a powerful facade concealing a process whereby flagship programmes were being produced with ever smaller teams of people. The irony was not lost on the

BBC workers inside the building, who noted when protestors chanted 'BBC where's your cameras?' that BBC Scotland's single available news camera was already in use, covering a story about ISIS. Writing in *Bella Caledonia,* publisher Adrian Searle related conversations with BBC staffers and pointed out, 'Those working inside the BBC complain that for opt-out programming screened in Scotland alone they are working with second class budgets and second class resources, while key editorial decisions are all made in London.'

As Bob Woodward, of Watergate fame once remarked, 'the best journalism is often done in defiance of management.' Real journalism often instinctively pushes against the structures it works within. While we can see the odd flicker of brilliance at BBC Scotland, whether from reports and documentaries by Alan Little or James Cook amongst others, or indeed the team behind the brilliantly candid post-referendum profile *Alex Salmond, a Rebel's Journey,* quality journalism did take place. Indeed, despite all of the problems that BBC Scotland faces, such coverage offers a glimpse of what a national broadcaster restored to its proper status could achieve.

In the meantime, BBC Scotland is often trapped in a kind of paralysis borne of the demands placed on it: held up on occasion as a mirror to a modern nation and at others derided as a purveyor of bland, embarrassingly small-minded local news content. It has never quite found its place in a shifting constitutional landscape. David Elstein, a former BBC producer and now an academic, is explicit in his description of just how centralised power is at the corporation:

The vast majority of the BBC's income - £3.6 billion from the licence fee, plus a further £1.5 billion gross and £150 million net from its commercial activities – is controlled

> from London in the shape of budgets for network tele-
> vision and radio channels, all of which are run from
> London (apart from Radio Five Live, which was moved to
> Salford, for entirely political reasons) … Like Edward the
> First in Wales, the BBC has built an impressive series of
> fortresses – Salford Quay, Pacific Quay – costing hundreds
> of millions of pounds, but these are as much an expres-
> sion of the BBC's power and how it exercises it as of any
> serious devolution of decision-making to the nations
> and regions.[134]

Improbable though it might seem, though it dare not speak its name, there is kind of a common cause amongst staff trapped within that large glass structure on the banks of the Clyde and those recently outraged at its output. In 2008 polling for the Scottish Broadcasting Commission found that out of 1,000 adults in Scotland, 81% of respondents said that they would be interested in watching a new television channel made for people living in Scotland. The highest level of demand for programmes on any new Scottish channel were for news programmes (58%), followed by documentaries (52%).[135] In contrast, the BBC's 2015 annual report found only 48% of Scots felt that their nation is effectively represented (eleven points below the UK average).[136] The BBC is about to enter into a process of tumultuous change. It is therefore imperative that Scotland stakes a claim as that process goes forward, not just for better Scottish broadcasting, but for the values embodied in public service broadcasting themselves, as they become threatened like never before. A re-think of what that concept means in a country that must unshackle itself from a bureaucratic and centralised past is deeply necessary. With a large minority of the population in Scotland set against the BBC and all that it stands for, it must radically reconsider its deeply unionist institutional structure, if it has any interest in re-engaging with public life in a contemporary nation still in the throes of rapid change. At the end of the day though, Scotland will not have better news coverage until it finds the political will to make it so and until the re-structuring process that ought to have been kick-started in the 1990s begins in earnest.

4

The Cultural Case

We want to go on faithfully telling Scotland's story. We want to go on being one of the main meeting-places where Scots come together to discuss their future. Pacific Quay is a test-bed for what the BBC could become, not just in technology but in creativity and the way people work together. It's our future.

> Mark Thompson, Speech given at opening of
> BBC Scotland's new headquarters at Pacific Quay[137]

For much of the last century, Scottish culture was the subject of a great deal of controversy. Did it exist? Should it exist? Could it flourish and develop, despite Scotland's lack of a state to call her own? Scottish cultural life, across a range of fields – from the visual and applied arts, to writing and drama – spent much of the twentieth century providing compelling responses to such questions. Scotland would see renaissance and revivals, the emergence of outstanding talent and a renewed sense of itself as a place with a diverse, dynamic and cosmopolitan culture.

Of course, that's just one version of a story that is far more complex and contested, but whatever else we might think about the current health of Scotland's arts and the country's 'creative industries' more generally, it's clear that across a range of media, a growing cultural confidence, a boldness of vision and a desire to explore Scottishness itself, is a definitive part of our recent history. In particular, cultural figures from a vast array of different backgrounds were seen to engage with Scottish public life. The work of countless writers, artists, theatre makers and musicians represents a culture that is self-aware, exploratory and outward looking. The salience of contemporary Scottish culture was perhaps best described by sociologist David McCrone in *Understanding Scotland*, 'The aim, it seems, is not to identify the unique Scottish experience, but to address the universal condition through day-to-day (Scottish) reality. The search for new images which express these experiences is no longer simply literary but artistic and cultural in the widest sense.' [138]

The roll call of artists and writers who contributed to this search is vast and includes those working in film and television: a list of actors, screenwriters, producers, directors and cinematographers that could match the output of any nation. Except it is in this area, perhaps uniquely in Scottish culture, that we encounter a glaring anomaly. If it is not too simplistic to assert that a successful country exports products, while a troubled one exports people, then, in this area at least, Scotland falls into the latter category. In terms of its screen culture, Scotland has left a meagre inheritance for aspiring talent that it has a dubious record at holding on to. Today's up-and-coming producers look out upon a scene defined by a dearth of opportunity: the result of major systemic failures. What makes this even more problematic is that the paucity of Scottish programming, particularly in areas like television drama, has long been defined by a frustratingly circular debate. Often, this consists of a seemingly endless chicken-and-egg argument that frequently blurs the line between cause – a lack of funding and political will – and effect: that very little original film or broadcasting is made in Scotland. In a set of notorious remarks at an OFCOM conference on public service broadcasting, in 2007, ITV's Chief Executive Michael Grade suggested that Scottish producers rarely obtained network commissions because 'they were not talented enough.' In response to a suggestion that some kind of quota system might be introduced to ensure more programmes were made in Scotland, Grade's reaction was uncompromising, 'I'm sorry to say that the money will follow the talent ... It's your problem, not my problem. You can't expect us to dish out money like sweeties because it's your turn.'[139]

Since 2007 there has been much talk of change, but very little in the way of concrete steps to develop a creative broadcasting industry in Scotland. The Scottish Broadcasting Commission's 2008 report and its flagship recommendation for a multi-million pound Scottish Digital Network, (with a public service remit to offer competition for BBC Scotland and STV), received broad support from across the political spectrum in Scotland. London, where the overwhelming majority of money still gets dished out, wasn't interested. Instead, the BBC's approach to broadcasting in Scotland is analogous to Britain's flawed post-war industrial policies. It is, like the Hillman Imp, a nominally 'Scottish' product, but with the crucial parts created by skilled workers in the south and shipped up. It's about fulfilling quotas rather than building a sustainable industry.

In this sense, the only sector that is still thirled to the bureaucratic anomalies of central planning in Britain is broadcasting. Nowhere can this be seen more clearly than in the response from the BBC to demands for more network television to be made in Scotland. A statistical target was set by Director General Mark Thompson in 2008: 9% of network programming would be made north of the border, 'We set ourselves a target of matching network supply from Scotland to Scotland's proportion of the United Kingdom's population by 2016.'[140] This remarkably literal approach to devolving programme making had controversial outcomes: the programmes that were allocated to the Scottish outpost were selected despite the fact that their content bore almost no relation to Scottish themes, ideas, concepts, writing or locations. The big-ticket programmes that ended up being produced under the banner of BBC Scotland, such as *Waterloo Road, Mrs Brown's Boys, Question Time,* and *Eggheads,* are not Scottish in any meaningful way. *Waterloo Road*, though widely praised for bringing jobs and training to Inverclyde, was a drama series specifically focused on the English school system. Re-setting the series in Greenock from Rochdale was perhaps the height of cultural mistranslation, resulting in a long running series being completely uprooted to Scotland via a somewhat spurious plot twist, trailed thus, 'On screen, the relocation will be played out in a "dramatic and explosive storyline"…this will see some of the current teachers and pupils at the troubled Rochdale comprehensive set up an independent school in Scotland.'[141] As an outraged *Manchester Evening News* reported, 'The bizarre plot has been compared to the *Dallas* storyline which saw Bobby Ewing brought back from the dead.'[142]

The presence of *Waterloo Road* is an exception to a pattern of steep decline in network drama output that originates in Scotland, on either BBC or STV. In 2009 the Association of Film and TV Producers Scotland (AFTPS) was set up 'in the face of growing levels of unemployment in the Scottish film and television industry,' with the stated aim of increasing Scottish-based TV commissioning, establishing production facilities, and to obtain greater levels of support and funding. In 2009 a survey of the 270 members of AFTPS found that 40% had less than 20 days work that year. Belle Doyle, a prominent member of the group, described the prevailing situation: 'there is not enough work to go around. What would be the optimum amount of work? Enough for people to get relevant experience, be paid proper rates for their work, and space for inexperienced crew to gain experience – so least one more medium-budget returning TV series with five or six features per year.'

Eleanor Yule, who worked as a producer for BBC Scotland in the 1990s, pinpoints the nature of Scotland's current production deficit, describing an 'urgent need' to increase 'Scottish-based commissioning of indigenous stories and original ideas', Yule claims:

> Editorial control for the majority of Scottish TV drama output still remains in London. The networks defend the lack of commissions of indigenously created content in Scotland by claiming that the ideas they receive from writers and independent companies based in Scotland are weaker than their original network competitors, which seems directly at odds with Scotland's global reputation for new prose fiction and the high percentage of award-winning Scottish radio plays by Scottish based writers on Radio Four.[143]

The hard truths of commissioning in the UK are vividly spelled out in a chapter in Yule's book with co-author David Manderston, *The Glass Half Full*, which recounts, amongst numerous examples of the narrowness of the Scotland on our screens, the difficulties that those trying to make original work in Scotland face. One anecdote tells of a London meeting with a BBC executive on the commissioning of a series about Charles Rennie Macintosh, in which it became apparent that the official in question had never heard of the renowned Scottish architect. Yule's conclusion is damning, 'The question must be asked: what is it the TV networks are actually looking for from Scotland? ... The evidence points to commissioning only ideas that originated in London or the two staples of Scottish fiction, miserablism and the kailyard.'[144] Such anomalies cannot, by definition, be solved by simply relocating pre-existing shows to Scotland. Instead, any meaningful solution must tackle the deep structural bias against original Scottish programming. For Ewan Crawford this is a critical question for the future of BBC Scotland:

It is part of the wider BBC organisation so there isn't a huge amount of independent decision making. When BBC Scotland does make programmes it's largely on an opt-out model and certainly if you take away *River City* ... if you look at peak time, it's not that you won't see very much output about from Scotland, you basically won't see any. In effect, there is no public sphere in relation to programming about Scotland during peak time and that is quite something given the prominence that any national broadcaster should have in a country. In my view that is unsustainable.

Robin MacPherson, Director of Screen Academy Scotland, also identifies the lack of original Scottish commissions as a symptom of the highly centralised structure under which the BBC still operates. Fundamentally, the incentive to make programmes for Scotland, about Scotland and addressing distinctive Scottish themes or concerns, does not register as a priority at a strategic level. This has created an almost inevitable 'talent drift' away from Scotland towards London:

The great thing about talent is that it can pop up anywhere ... you can't predict where it will pop up, but you can corral it and bring it down and train it ... the stuff that you create, is part of a menu that provides the colour in a predominantly metropolitan way of looking at the world. And as long as the film making and cultural and commissioning power resides in London, of course that's what you have. And that's the relationship that we've had ever since the BBC was established.

The images of Scotland that are presented on big and small screen, especially if they are destined for UK wide audiences, are almost certain to conform to certain tried and tested formats, genres, or versions of Scotland that are easily translatable beyond the country's borders. This means that for writers, actors or producers working in Scotland there is often, somewhat perversely, a need to over-state their Scottishness or the Scottish brand that accompanies their offering, in a manner that would not be required in a more home-grown, mature, broadcasting culture. Scotland is essentially still a region when it comes to broadcasting. This is not simply restricted to the creative sector. Iain Macwhirter, who fronted BBC programmes in London and Scotland, believes that there is a tendency to apply lower quality production values in the north:

> BBC Scotland is made to look regional – it doesn't happen by accident. I presented directly comparable political television programmes for network and for Scotland: the thrice-weekly *Westminster Live* in the 1990s and *Holyrood Live* in the 2000s. The latter started off in a radio studio. It had less than a third of the staff and no dedicated camera crews. This inevitably showed on air. It's why BBC Scotland programmes just 'feel' second rate. When I complained I was told: "Scotland has a tenth of the population so you only get a tenth of the budget." The problem here is that while there are many talented people in BBC Scotland the programmes are not benchmarked to network standards. This is a kind of struc-tural mediocrity, and completely unjustifiable following Scotland's democratic renewal. Why should programmes be inferior just because they are Scottish?

Nothing but Heather (and heroin)

Tom Nairn's seminal work on constitutional politics and culture in the UK, *The Break up of Britain*, introduced several provocative terms for understanding how Scotland, a 'sub-national' entity, long occupied a status somewhere between region and nation. Noting the effect this had on culture as defined by 'a huge, virtually self-contained universe of *Kitsch*'[145] Nairn claims the country is the victim of a 'tartan monster', a set of clichéd and limited representations, for which Nairn coined the term 'tartanry':

> The Scottish masses were not socialised into a unitary national culture. Inevitably they were forced to compose for themselves a bastard product that was part 'indigenous' - expressing the still quite different life and social ethic of the country - and part Great British or imperialist. Thus, the ultra-patriotism of tartanry is accompanied by a tradition of sentimentalised savagery which reflected Scotland's participation in two centuries of Great British exploits, in the subjugation of many genuine 'subject nations'.[146]

Across swathes of Scottish culture, tartanry has been mocked, banished, re-imagined and interrogated. Contemporary artist Rachel McLean's work, for example, is based on a fantasia of tartan-clad imagery. It is no longer a fraught and insular search for a 'unitary culture' to make up for generations of cringe, but one about many Scotlands. As such, that smaller, parochial Scotland: singular in either its quaint folksy charms or the 'miserablism' of the contemporary 'urban kailyard' and 'tartan noir' staples, no longer provokes the extreme adoration or revulsion that it once did. Instead, we can reflect that much has been done in numerous fields to show a Scotland of multitudes and varieties: a project at home in a world in which borders of nation states are porous and in which globalisation has come to play a part in every aspect of our cultural existence. Few parts of Scottish life have failed to embrace this notion that Scotland is something more than just a provincial backwater or romanticised oddity trapped in the past, whether rural or industrial. There is however, one frequent exception: the Scotland that we seen on our screens.

Take for example the much vaunted arrival of a new current affairs programme, *Scotland 2014/15*, a move that replaced the *Newsnight Scotland* opt-out with a beefed up offering. For the most part, its format remains dull and unimaginative, and it is rarely prepared to step out from the straightjacket of devolved issues and the Holyrood political bubble. A quick comparison with *Newsnight* (the programme it opts-out of) is illustrative: everything, from the size of the studio, to the lighting and the range of the topics covered, is tangibly inferior. Most cringingly of all perhaps, visual cues about Scotland abound in the opening credits. Unlike the sombre, abstract and powerful tones of *Newsnight*, viewers of *Scotland 2014/15* are given a visual pick-and-mix of glossy Scotch characters and objects: a Tunnocks caramel wafer, a set of bagpipes, an Edinburgh tram, a can of Irn Bru, the Glenfinnan Viaduct, Andy Murray, a west highland terrier and Edinburgh Castle (to name just a few). This need to differentiate a Scottish programme, via obvious cultural symbols, says far more about those creating the media product than those consuming it, and this is one of the most important points that Scotland needs to remember about its deficient media. Scotland must, time and time again, be made more singular, via a reductive process of identifying it via clichés, awkward bonhomie and symbols of its past. Reversing the contrast with *Newsnight* is I think, illustrative. Could we ever imagine the UK's flagship current affairs programme opening with a collage featuring a pint of bitter, Morris dancers, the London Underground, David Beckham and Buckingham Palace? Expressions of superiority are always about a need to single out the lesser creation, to mark it out as more particular and less universal. No other serious news programme in any nation in the world would open with *kitsch* symbolic reminders of its provenance.

The assumption that Scots are suckers for national symbols has little basis in fact. What's more, though it may simply feel pleasing to state, it is entirely unclear for whose benefit Scottishness is so blatantly identified at certain points on air. Perhaps the idea is that by being so profoundly Scottish on certain occasions, broadcasters feel such content can act like a kind of protein supplement, packing in an artificially high dose of identity to distract from the lack of nourishment elsewhere.

Contrary to what the British establishment might think today, Scotland is not and never has been a particularly nationalistic country in any sense. Its history of cultural cringe is perhaps a testament to this, representing, as it does, a form of struggle to reconcile an authentic Scottish identity with hard political realities. The contemporary surge in national feeling was really a product of the 1980s, a modern, self-aware and often deeply political response to mass changes brought about by Thatcherism. This reassertion of Scottishness was often urban, subversive and radical. It was also remarkably broad: taking in pop music, theatre, literature, traditional music, visual art, and yes, film and broadcasting too. Throughout the 1970s and 80s, an array of programmes, including numerous drama series, were made by BBC Scotland for the network. As Eleanor Yule describes it, 'The whole of Scotland was represented on television, across all classes, not just the central belt and not just Glasgow.' [147] The era referred to includes that overseen by Pharic Maclaren, who regularly placed Scottish drama on the BBC network (including a renowned adaptation of *Sunset Song*) and original Scottish classics such as John Byrne's *Tutti Frutti*.

Without even the presence of Glasgow's most prolific sleuth on our screens any more (*Taggart* was axed in 2011), the capacity of Scottish broadcasters to tell any kind of story about the country they serve is severely limited. As Teddy Jamieson pointed out in an eloquent essay in relation to the 2011 Scottish BAFTAs, 'the danger is that broadcasting timidity leads to cultural repetition. And repetition leads to a cultural reductiveness,' adding, 'There's a curious disconnect between the increasing self-confidence of Scots on a political level and the hermetic, defeatist programmes we watch.'[148]

In adopting the sub-national mindset, broadcasters often seem to assume that a Scottish audience will want Scottish things, and that therefore programming about Scotland is a particular and fairly limited niche, a special interest, reserved largely for staged events: a Hogmanay special, a Burns night, a sporting contest, a festival. These are the staples of big budget programming in Scotland but they do not amount to a sustained and creative engagement with the rest of modern Scottish culture. That the BBC has a duty to reflect the vibrancy of the Scottish arts, mainstream and alternative, is self-evident: as it is fond of claiming, the corporation is the biggest cultural organisation in the country. But it is often, like Nairn's cultural sub-nationalism, 'curiously fixed or fossilised.' The narrower, more singular Scotland that we so often see on screen, is trapped by the need to regurgitate the limited mix of genres and formats that are available to it. Unable to look beyond into the wider, more exciting global scene (interaction with global audiences must still be mediated through London) it is trapped both by the past and the lack of freedom to explore what the country currently is and might become: surely the most important function of culture anywhere.

With *Waterloo Road* now finished, the Glasgow based soap-opera, *River City*, has become the only long running TV drama series produced in Scotland. *River City's* creator Stephen Greenhorn, whose credits as a screenwriter also include *Sunshine on Leith*, *Glasgow Kiss* and episodes of *Doctor Who*, explains the importance of the soap:

It does mean that there is a possibility of sustainable employment for all those people that work in the Scottish TV industry. If that evaporates, if *River City* stops ... and there's nothing else in there to keep a certain momentum, then all those people will go. Once they've gone the chances of being able to push towards a Welsh style renaissance are that much harder.

Greenhorn's reference to Wales touches on an important point. Scotland has consistently fallen behind its near neighbours in terms of both film and TV production. Creative Scotland, which had £4 million to spend on film in 2013/14, oversees a budget significantly smaller than that of both Northern Ireland (£12 million) and the Republic of Ireland (£14 million). The 'Welsh renaissance', has succeeded in establishing a £30 million tranche of funding managed in association with Pinewood, who last year founded a major studio in Wales aimed at film and high-end TV drama.[149] In large part built off the back of the success of Russell T. Davies' revival of *Doctor Who* and its spin off *Torchwood*, Cardiff has become a hub for programme making, a legacy that has been lauded for having 'left its own inspirational mark on the nation's imagination and the economy of his own homeland's capital city.'[150] Scotland, in contrast, missed out on the opportunity to host *Game of Thrones* to Northern Ireland because of a 'lack of quality studio space.'[151] While plans are underway to build a dedicated film studio in Scotland, voices from within the industry in January 2015 complained of the lack of leadership in the form of a single dedicated film agency. John Archer, chair of Independent Producers Scotland told a committee of the Scottish Parliament, 'What we want to see is the Scottish Government set a screen policy, informed by producers and the various agencies, which says: "This is what we expect of you over this next few years."'[152] Long running issues about studio space and the viability of a dedicated commercial film studio also continue to hold back Scotland's potential status as a serious player in the industry. 'A studio – or indeed any kind of dedicated professional production space – is a way of showing that Scotland is a place to make feature films and high-end returning TV series,' says Belle Doyle, while gesturing to the underlying anxieties that have held back such a project, 'The irony is that no Scottish feature film could actually afford to use any studio space, but people realise that it's really important for inward investment (and this would have a knock-on effect in developing the industry here),' she adds.

The point, as Greenhorn picks up, is to get a kind of critical mass of production taking place across the board in Scotland, as has occurred in Wales, 'We need to get to a point where there's enough companies based up here that you'd actually need to have good reason *not to be* shooting in Scotland, rather than a reason *to be* shooting in Scotland,' says Greenhorn.

All of Scotland is Our Stage

As David McCrone has pointed out, the debate kicked off by Tom Nairn is essentially an 'internalist' one and can seem increasingly at odds in a world where singular national identity is becoming increasingly fluid and the idea of homogenous national culture is seen as increasingly elusive.[153] The really pertinent questions about Scottish screen culture and its status are external, about its relationship and ability to interact across national boundaries, with its neighbours, and across the globe. Such a global agenda is obviously complicated by a metropolis that is close by, but increasingly off-limits to those trying to make a living in the arts. In this sense, London's dominance is not simply legislative, financial and structural. It has long dominated the UK cultural sector as a major global city and Scotland's proximity to it has often provoked tensions about the way in which a country with half its population, only a five hour train journey away, can compete. Without major public intervention, it can't compete, but nonetheless must maintain a guarded ability to host culture on its own terms. Arts journalist Andrew Eaton Lewis has seen this at work in a range of fields:

> I can think of countless times, in my years as arts editor for the *Scotsman* and, latterly, *Scotland on Sunday*, when significant cultural events in Scotland – things I would put on a magazine front page without hesitation – were virtually ignored by the London media, while things of little relevance to anyone outside London were lavished with attention.

Cultural capital is unevenly distributed throughout Britain, and like its financial equivalent, clawing it back has never been easy. Eaton-Lewis found this closely aligned to his native north of England thanks to, 'a sensibility partly shaped ... by being marginalised by a political, economic and cultural establishment all run from London.'[154]

What is most remarkable is that, despite all of London's clout as a global city, even the UK film industry has struggled to define itself amid fierce international competition. The current battle over the future of the BBC and its role as a producer demonstrates that despite the UK's unrivalled 'soft power' it has also lost something of its edge in TV drama, as Armando Ianucci pointed out at the 2015 Edinburgh International Television Festival, 'The best US shows are modelling themselves on what used to make British TV so world-beating.'[155] In an era defined by the 'boxed set' series as pioneered by HBO in America, the importance of TV drama as major narrative art has never been greater. With highly popular, critically acclaimed series like *The Wire* and *Boardwalk Empire*, or DR's *The Killing* and *Borgen*, the absence of even the possibility of long running, serious and innovative indigenous Scottish TV drama is particularly glaring. The BBC's *Wolf Hall* (2015) is of a similar order, but where, we might ask, could we begin to look for a Scottish alternative? The answer is that it already exists, in a very direct sense, it's just not on screen. The staging of Rona Munro's *The James Plays* (2014) by NTS was also hailed as a landmark cultural achievement. Like *Wolf Hall*, it focused on the country's dynastic past, boasted a stellar cast and presented compelling drama and vividly drawn characters. The play's executive producer, Neil Murray, commenting on its impending revival for international audiences in 2016 noted, 'the "box-set" version of theatre watching is evidently now an attractive option for people seeking an exhilarating, intense entertainment experience.'[156] That a play focusing on a hitherto obscure aspect of pre-modern Scottish history could become an international hit, is a reminder that while Scotland is consistently able to stage its narrative imagination, it can only rarely be glimpsed on screen.

Modern theatre in Scotland therefore provides an interesting point of comparison. The National Theatre of Scotland (NTS), a 'theatre without walls' was founded after years of campaigning and innovation in Scottish theatre. Its ethos is distinctively post-national, and its tagline 'all of Scotland is our stage, and on that stage we perform to the world' is as succinct as it is bold. It is a very significant framing of a national institution that sought, from its inception, to be decentralised and accessible rather than elitist and cloistered. Though it has known detractors since it was founded in 2006, the company has managed to achieve significant international acclaim. Noting the international success of NTS productions like *Black Watch* Stephen Greenhorn contrasts the different commissioning cultures within the theatre and screen sectors:

> ...if you want to raise your country's visibility on the world stage, then *Black Watch* is a fucking gift ... with a spritely imaginative commissioning system within Scottish telly they could have done what Vicky [Featherstone] did ... to

say, we think there's something there, can you stay on that
story and see if there's something there? But it's the fear-
fulness, the first question they'd ask is, would the network
want that? And the whole thing starts to evaporate after
that.

When we consider Scotland's thriving music and visual arts
scenes, its claim to one of the best known literary traditions in the
world and a proven ability to host world class events, our film
and TV deficit seem all the more astonishing. The success of the
live arts in Scotland is perhaps best exemplified by the Edinburgh
festivals which, as critic Joyce McMillan vociferously argued at the
Changin Scotland Festival in March 2015, have had a totally transformative effect how Scottish culture sees itself:

I think it is genuinely difficult to imagine, now, how we
would see Edinburgh and how we would see Scotland
itself if it didn't have this International Festival, with
the Fringe still much the biggest international festival
in Europe happening every year. The way it has brought
international artists into Scotland, artists who have experienced that work have been inspired and have felt that
they have had international connections, not depending
on having to go through London or the British government. So long before political power was devolved back to
Edinburgh this powerhouse of cultural energy was coming
there every year, inspiring and empowering Scottish based
artists, giving them a whole international dimension to
their lives.[157]

McMillan's point about political power is a cogent one. As could be
seen in the achievement of Glasgow's 1990 City of Culture status,
a very conscious bid to use 'soft power' to revive post-industrial

Scotland was transformative. It changed the face of the country and rebooted its sense of itself as a place that could engage with other cultures and express itself to the world on its own terms. Arguably this served to set the agenda for the political devolution that was to follow. This also occurred off the back of at least a decade of a new found interest in Scottish culture, exemplified by the work of Alasdair Gray, Irvine Welsh, John Byrne, Liz Lochhead, James Kelman, Ken Currie, Edwin Morgan, Janice Galloway, Ian Hamilton Finlay and numerous others. Such well-wrought effort to imagine the nation had a well-documented and profound impact. But their imaginative project was not nationalist, beyond the basic sense that the nation is a key space for such activity, as critic Cairns Craig points out, 'The nation "imagines" because it is the nation through which the agency of human groups is primarily exerted in the modern world.'[158] Perhaps with an eye on this inheritance, a strong rhetorical commitment to culture continued into the devolution years. The Scottish Executive's 2005 Cultural Commission report opens with remarks from First Minister Jack McConnell of utopian proportions:

> In the 20th Century it took immense courage and political resolve to deliver universal health care and school education for all. Today these rights are unquestioned, pillars of modern society. I believe we can now make the development of our creative drive, our imagination, the next major enterprise for our society.... I believe this has the potential to be a new civic exercise on a par with health, housing and education.[159]

Whether or not such lofty aims were ever able to be delivered, they demonstrate the vital importance that politicians of all stripes in Scotland seem prepared to attribute to Scotland's culture. In 2013 Fiona Hyslop made a conscious effort to distance the Scottish Government from its Westminster counterpart's desire to link cultural subsidy to economic growth, stating, 'We actively support the case for public subsidy of the arts. We understand that culture and heritage have a value in and of themselves.'[160] However, the question of whether such rhetoric can be matched with concrete policies to revitalise film and TV in Scotland remains to be seen. Beyond the desire to see broadcasting devolved and a greater share of the licence fee spent in Scotland, creative ideas for the renewal of these industries will require a major re-alignment of current political priorities.[161] With little in terms of quality or subject matter to mark them out, the essential difference between the production that delivered *Wolf Hall* to a prime time television audience and the *James Plays* to theatre-goers is the former's £7 million price tag.

As the best international examples show, time, patience and money are key. On top of its film funding, Denmark's reputation for quality drama is underpinned by one of the best-funded public service broadcasters in the world, affording writers and actors the space to develop characters and scripts.[162] The quality high-end drama still available from across the Atlantic would never have been possible without innovations in financing. The second golden age of American TV was built on a new funding model, the development of subscription only channels that, '... shaped a creative space similar to American independent cinema – allowing subject-matter, language and action that the ancient studios would have cut – but with a more fixed supply of funding and audiences.'[163]

Perhaps the lack of linguistic nationalism obscures the significance of national film and broadcasting. The existential utility of Scottish productions seems more politicised (in a way that BBC Alba for example, is not). Henrik Bo Nielsen of the Danish National Film Institute explained the importance of the sector to his own country: 'We think it is important that Danes are told stories about themselves and in their language.' With decades of commitment to the national industry, the Danes can expect around 25 feature dramas and 30 documentaries a year to be made in their native land. The annual budget for Danish film is around £65 million per year. A nation with virtually the same population as Scotland, spending over ten times as much public money on film.[164]

Perhaps the problem is about internal anxieties about Scotland's ability to deliver quality output. The most respected Scottish film-maker of all time, John Grierson, the 'father of the documentary' was sceptical about the viability of a Scottish film industry.[165] Such a lack of confidence has led to decades of stasis. Robin MacPherson has pointed out that the crisis in Scottish film-making is older than most people who work in it, noting that still unmet calls for a Scottish film studio were first made in the 1930s.[166] 'The interesting thing about the state of the media in Scotland is how little concern it really arouses amongst the chattering classes … Actually it's part of what you might call a 'small u' general unionist, global, metropolitan outlook,' says McPherson, before gesturing to the complexities of addressing the current structural media deficit, 'as with any other under-representation, unless you take serious positive action to redress a strong structural imbalance, whatever the reasons for that strong structural imbalance, you can't expect the situation to change.'

Conclusion

In 2011 Andrew O'Hagan neatly encapsulated Scotland's capacity to re-imagine itself by stating 'If Scotland is parochial, then it's a parochialism that has changed the world.'[167] It echoes Patrick Kavanagh's point that, 'Parochialism is universal; it deals with the fundamentals.'[168] The cultural case for a Scottish media is premised on the need for a vision in the first instance of what Scotland actually wants to see on its screens. This is necessary to make the benefits clear for a process that would amount to vast structural changes and an entire re-thinking of the place of culture within Scottish politics. Decades of fine rhetoric must be translated into a plan for action, now. Contemporary Scottish culture doesn't need to re-iterate itself, yet often this is all that the country's negligible film and TV sector is able to offer. Broadcasting is something that has happened in or to Scotland, it has only occasionally occurred in Scotland's interests. This is not normal. We need to begin from the ground up and understand that the scope of necessary change is vast and foundational. Could we begin to assert the right of Scots to tell stories to each other, in any medium, about who we are in a manner unfettered by metropolitan diktat? That a distinct culture ought to have its own properly structured public sphere in the form of control over commissioning, a properly supported film industry and drastically increased levels of investment, seems self-evident. Too often, we think of culture as a product or an industry when it is in fact a process, that impacts on every walk of life, from the tenor of our laws to the shape of our cities. Such an ethos was at the heart of a 'Cultural Affirmation' put forward in May 2015 by Traditional Arts and Culture Scotland, which stated, 'Scotland's artists and cultural workers have a right to inform, influence and where necessary to own the means of cultural production and dissemination in their individual and collective interest.'[169] That such a statement is so far from its realisation does not make it radical. Cultural capital, 'soft power' is transformative and it is time we resolved to make a claim for it.

If we want Scottish culture to fulfil its capacity to make content that is enjoyed both at home and abroad, we need to establish a basic minimum level of Scottish programming, not based on an arbitrary statistical target, but starting instead from a broad and substantive conversation premised on the need to see modern Scotland represented in all its diversity. When Bill Forsyth made his timeless ode to growing up in Scotland, *Gregory's Girl*, he responded to those who were startled by its success by noting, 'There were five million people living in Scotland who had rarely seen their lives on the cinema screen.'[170] That is, in a sense, one of the most basic statements of the case for a Scottish media. It is also among the most compelling.

5

Being Thought Independent

The sandstone building, which stands high above Edinburgh's Waverley Station, glaring down from the city's Old
Town, was constructed on the principle that the highest
and most abstract parts of the business took place at the
top and as you descended, floor by floor, the physical side
took over ... until you came to the Linotype operators and
the intoxicating sweet stench of newsprint and the rumble
and heat of the presses. Eventually, as originally designed,
the freshly printed, cut, folded and rolled-up parcels of
newspaper would fall out of the building's stone anus into
a waiting railway truck - the line actually went into the
basement of the building - and be whisked away across
Scotland hot for the breakfast tables of lawyers, GPs and
ministers of the kirk.

Andrew Marr, *My Trade*[171]

The old *Scotsman* building is a monument to the high-esteem in
which the Scottish press was once held. Few newspaper buildings anywhere in the world can boast an imposing grandeur to
match that which stands above the teeming streets of central
Edinburgh. Those wishing to catch a glimpse of the historic
status of the Scottish press need only glance up at it from North
Bridge or Princes Street. Yet, like many of Edinburgh's architec-

tural gems, it is now little more than a historic curio. In a city increasingly fond of selling off its remarkable built environment to the highest bidder, to become luxury hotels (like the *Scotsman* building) it is now more akin to one of the massive tombstones in the Old Calton Cemetery just across the bridge: a monument to that which is no more. The colourful, bustling, picture painted by Marr in his memoir is now long gone: for all its vivid sensory appeal it is a description of a Scotland that has passed. Today, the *Scotsman* is based on the fringes of the city centre at Orchard Brae House, after it had to ditch a second purpose-built headquarters on Holyrood Road. The £20m structure, opened in 1999 by the Queen, had space for 600 employees. The paper's current staff, now pooled across its sister titles, is only a fraction of that number. When the building was handed over to games developer Rock Star North it was expected to save Johnston Press as much as £1m per year.[172] Such legacy costs, left over from the good years at the turn of the century, have a lot to answer for when it comes to considering how far Scottish newspapers have fallen. Stewart Kirkpatrick, editor of scotsman.com from 2000-2007, described the deeply troubled state in which the paper now finds itself: 'The impression I get is that it's not a happy place to work and there is a sense of a whittling way, of trimming beyond the bone and of an endless round of cuts. People tend to be very proud of the titles they work for and to defend them, but the impression I get from people I speak to is that they find it harder and harder to take pride in the paper.'

The proud and pervasive title that Marr describes was not only the training ground for countless leading journalists, it was also an intricately woven part of the fabric of Scotland's national life. Often that national life was corseted, narrow and elitist, but the esteem with which the *Scotsman* was held, its reputation for quality and high literary standards, gave the paper a voice that was respected and listened to well beyond the breakfast tables of Morningside and Trinity. On one level, the decline of the *Scotsman* is the decline of the version of the Scottish establishment that it represented. It has, like church attendance, a certain decrepit inevitability about it. Its story is part of a wider narrative, about the decline of institutions that were once at the heart of Scottish society and identity. But this did not happen overnight. Crass decisions, acute misjudgements and notable failures to ride the waves of change that have swept over Scotland in recent decades have seen what was once a truly national paper retreat from that status and into decline. It is easy to look at such developments with the benefit of hindsight and the indifferent shrug of formerly loyal readers after they've had enough. But to do so is to forget a story about how one of the few crucial spaces for the expression of Scottish civic identity was so easily misappropriated, mismanaged and neglected.

If we look back, beyond the dwindling pagination and successive rounds of redundancies, a distinct heritage and a story about the significant role of the newspaper and its development in Scotland can be seen. This is an aspect of Scottish history which is often presented as little more than a footnote: yet the nation's press has been profoundly influential in shaping the country that we know today. Arguably, the Scottish press acted as one of the main institutional 'carriers' of Scottish distinctiveness in a stateless nation. In 1994 Maurice Smith, in his book, *Paper Lions*, expounded on the role of the Scottish press as a medium that expressed national identity, 'That need to proclaim our difference as Scots is channelled through our press … Just as Scotland feels it deserves a "national" identity, it wishes to see its press as "national" in the same terms. Newspapers (and for that matter broadcasters) actually require the distinction, in order to identify themselves as something more than "regional"'.[173]

Historically Scotland's awkward 'sub-national' status was problematic on a number of fronts, but it was successful in maintaining Scotland as a distinct entity. Its press, along with other institutions, like the Kirk and the law, displayed a 'Scottish accent of mind' that was crucial to sustaining its distinctiveness within the union. Even at the height of the British Empire, Scottish national identity was articulated throughout the press with an intensity equal to that of any independent nation.[174] Given this context, it seems remarkable that last year's referendum saw only one title, the *Sunday Herald*, 'come out' in support of Scottish independence. Why was a view that came to be expressed by 45% of voters, on a massive turnout, treated with seemingly inexhaustible reserves of editorial incredulity? As every daily leader writer in Scotland penned their endorsement for the union, was there not concern that they would all, as a body, seem out of touch with a substantial number of Scots? Or was the value of the union, culturally, politically and commercially, simply too great to risk?

The Scottish press is an old institution, creaking under the weight of centuries, it does not, we must presume, make decisions about Scotland's future lightly. It does not alarm its readers without a sense of due cause and alarming headlines came thick and fast in 2014. So to understand why this crucial forum, this public sphere, performed its democratic task with such stunning uniformity we must go back to look at that the role print played in Scotland historically. Printing predates the union and like all other societies its arrival and development is of great importance. The North Bridge temple to the newspaper, with its 'massive, sepulchral dignity' and all its dirty, booze soaked glory, may be an oddity today.[175] Like the country's heavy industries it is largely confined to nostalgic, overwhelmingly masculine, memories and is equally out of kilter with contemporary Scotland. But, as with all print cultures, whatever its future, the newspaper in Scotland will continue to leave an indelible mark on the character of the place.

Origins: Print in Scotland

Jack Goody has argued that oral cultures, lacking the ability to trap ideas in a fixed format, have what is described as 'structural amnesia' – in that they remember the past as if it were like the present.[176] The capturing of words, ideas, memories and narratives in permanent black and white form is a radically transformative moment in the history of our species. It is also worth reflecting that, from the printing press to the web, the arrival of new media technologies has invariably been greeted with a mixture of utopian optimism from below and abject horror from above. Those who enjoyed the status of gatekeepers before the new technology came into use are often deeply troubled by new arrivals that undermine such control.

This is why the fundamental shift represented by the invention of the printing press by Johannes Gutenberg in 1440 is accorded such a seminal place in history. With that single development, the power of the religious establishment of the day to tightly control the dissemination of knowledge was overturned. Gutenberg's press was significantly faster than the process of block printing used in East Asia for centuries and vastly outpaced the copyists of medieval monasteries in Europe. The effects were, quite literally, revolutionary. The pre-eminent mind in the field of media studies, Marshall McLuhan, succinctly captures the significance of this historic moment, 'With Gutenberg Europe enters the technological phase of progress, when change itself becomes the archetypal norm of social life.'[177]

The first printing press arrived in Scotland in 1508: and it was just around the corner from the site of the iconic *Scotsman* building, in the Edinburgh's Cowgate, that printing in Scotland was born. It was here that burgesses Walter Chepman and Andrew Millar set up their printing operation.[178] Crucially, some of the first texts printed by Chepman and Millar were in the vernacular language:

not Latin, but Scots (examples of which survive today and are held by the National Library of Scotland). It is in these documents, marked with the distinctive ornamental devices of the two men, that we see the first green shoots of a print culture in Scotland: the impact of which would be of profound importance to the development of early modern Scottish society. As a northern European country, Scotland would become profoundly altered by print and hardwired into the intellectual life of a Europe thrown into flux by decades of religious conflict. When Scotland experienced the full of force of the revolutionary tide of the Reformation in the sixteenth century, the role of literacy became critical. Scotland's (sometimes disputed) achievement of higher levels of literacy than England is often attributed to the religious zeal that John Knox and others brought back from the continent. While some have argued that there is a lack of hard evidence to prove Scotland was a particularly literate society at this time, we do know that there is a long tradition of portraying it as such. The statistician, Sir John Sinclair, renowned for his creation of the Statistical Account of Scotland, summed up this sentiment in 1826:

> ...the great body of the people in the more southern part of Scotland, having very generally obtained the blessings of education, the art of reading and writing, and a knowledge of the elements of arithmetic, in those districts, have been placed within the reach of almost every individual; while persons of all ranks, being taught to read the Bible from their earliest years, and being instructed in the catechisms ... have received the rudiments of a religious education, such as they could not have had the same means of obtaining, in almost any other country.[179]

The importance of words, and the knowledge bound up in them, may have been hammered into Scotland's psyche by the tumult of centuries of religious upheaval following the reformation and the 'killing times' of the Covenanters. It was, after all, the imposition of an unwanted religious text, *The Book of Common Prayer,* upon a disgruntled Scottish congregation that sparked a series of events that would eventually lead to the war and revolution throughout the British Isles in the 17th century. In Scotland, a country that quite literally bled in order to read its chosen good book without let or hinderance, information trapped in paper and ink took on sacred status.

The Public Sphere

By the Act of Union in 1707, a vibrant print culture had sprung up that engaged with the pressing issue of the day with eloquence and satirical wit in a variety of forms. As Leith Davis has argued, the high political drama of union saw a surge in print that extended the reach of political rhetoric and the oral debate to the wider populace: 'The union debate was accompanied by an unprecedented amount of printed material. But, like the 2014 referendum debates, the 1707 debates also afford a view of the interaction between old and new media.'[180] Post-union the newfound distance from central government helped facilitate the first flourishing of newspapers north of the border. With the exception of the short lived *Mercurius Caledonius* (1661) (regarded as the first Scottish newspaper worthy of the name) the development of the newspaper in Scotland had to wait until the abolition of the repressive Scottish Privy Council in 1708. Though several early newspaper titles such as the *Edinburgh Evening Courant* (1781-1871) and *The Caledonian Mercury* (1720-1867) are no longer with us, a surprising number of the first Scottish papers are still in print. The oldest survivor is Aberdeen's *Press and Journal* (1748) while the *Glasgow Advertiser/Herald* (1783-), Dundee's *Courier*

(1816-), the *Scotsman* (1817-) and the *Inverness Courier* (1817-) are all a ripe old age.[181]

The link between such publications and the multimedia world we inhabit today may seem remote, but the legacy of these products is still with us in more ways than one. As sociologist Jürgen Habermas has argued, throughout Western Europe, this new print culture helped to create the 'public sphere': an arena for rational civic engagement with topical matters. The emergence of newspapers, along with their often active, letter writing, readerships represented something entirely new: a wide community drawn together across geographic and even social divides. As a result a novel concept developed: that of public opinion, a term which is first recorded in French around 1750, in English in 1781 and in German in 1793.[182] In Habermas's influential work *The Structural Transformation of the Public Sphere* (1962) he describes the central concept thus: 'In its clash with the arcane and bureaucratic practices of the absolutist state, the emergent bourgeoisie gradually replaced a public sphere in which the ruler's power was merely represented before the people with a sphere in which state authority was publicly monitored through informed and critical discourse by the people.'[183]

That use of discourse, taking place in a public space, separate from authority but able to interact with it, was crucial, necessary even, for a certain basic level of participation in politics: it underpins the values that we attribute to a functioning 'fourth estate' today. The importance of new communication technology and standardised vernacular languages to the development of modern polities cannot be underestimated. Often early newspapers were self-consciously communicating with an 'imagined' community of like minded readers, in a manner that had a direct link to the contemporary oral cultures of coffee houses and debating clubs. Probably the most well known example, the *Spectator*, was originally founded around the concept of an entirely fictitious 'Spectator Club'. As technology improved, increasingly large groups of readers were able to converse on a range of subjects, and the growing size and diversity of readership was of profound significance. Thanks to the intellectual reputation of Scotland in the late eighteenth century and the crucial role of Edinburgh in the enlightenment's 'republic of letters' via organs such as the pioneering *Edinburgh Review,* Scotland became a renowned exporter of media products. This helped to sustain, nurture and broaden the sense of participation in a national community. The popularity of Sir Walter Scott throughout Europe was of great importance to Scotland's reputation as an unrivalled producer of men of letters and as a centre for publishing. The effect of Scott's novels throughout Europe created a kind of international cultural capital for Scotland that is analogous to that enjoyed by Hollywood blockbuster films today.

The rise of the newspaper, on the other hand, had to wait for archaic legislation to fall before it could get established. In Britain the activities of the press were deliberately restricted by a range of taxes from 1712 onwards. As a result circulation was severely limited and prosecutions against the proprietors of radical papers who refused to submit to the stamping system were frequent. This draconian regime resulted in a situation by the 1830s in which hundreds of periodicals and newspapers were circulating illegally. Such radical publications had a particular appeal in a city like Glasgow with its vast urban proletariat. In this period, it was to become a centre for social activism and the home of publications such as the *Loyal Reformer's Gazette* (1831-8) the *Scottish Trades Union Gazette* (1833) and the *Tradesman* (1833-4). Alexander Campbell, who owned the *Tradesman*, considered 'the founding father of the Scottish labour movement,' was charged with evading duty and, despite payment, was convicted.[184]

Print Capitalism

With the emergence of what Benedict Anderson terms 'print-capitalism' in the nineteenth century, we reach a fascinating stage in Scotland's media journey. By the nineteenth century, as Anderson argues in *Imagined Communities* (1983) newspapers contributed to the formation of national consciousness by treating their readers as a community, a national public.[185] Wealth at home, premised on an early start in the industrial revolution thanks to plentiful supplies of coal and iron in close proximity to water, created a society sophisticated enough to develop one of the world's strongest print industries.[186] It was also an era of civic pride, when the autonomous institutions of the Scottish establishment reigned supreme, with minimal interference from central government. As was the case throughout Britain, the abolition of stamp-duty on newspapers in 1855 was a pivotal moment for the burgeoning fourth estate, celebrated in verse by a contributor to the *Manchester Guardian* thus:

> To day the press, from duty free,
> Appears on every side;
> Whilst competition reigns around,
> And news is scattered wide.
> A perfect flood of papers rise,
> Like breakers in the storm,
> Of every size - at every price -
> And every make and form.[187]

The effects of this legislative change would be accelerated by development of the railway system. The newspaper industry in Britain, already centred on Fleet Street, saw a period of rapid expansion. In England, the transformative effect of this technology for newspapers overwhelmingly favoured London based titles. The reason only a very small number of regional English morning papers have survived, such as the *Yorkshire Post* (Leeds) or the *Western Mail* (Cardiff) is seen as a direct result of the railways allowing newspapers from the capital to take advantage of a massively expanded and speedy distribution network. Yet thanks to geography, this did not hurt Scottish titles, as David Hutchison explains:

> Paradoxically, Scotland's newspapers benefited from the limitations of the railway system ... it was difficult for newspaper trains to reach Scotland in time for the titles to be on sale alongside the Scottish ones. Even when printing centres linked through telecommunications systems to London were opened in the north of England, distribution problems remained. Scottish newspapers were given a long breathing space not available to their English provincial counterparts in which to build up reader loyalty. All four of the country's major cities acquired significant press industries and, despite the predominance of Glasgow based titles, retain them today.[188]

In an era when newspapers became an indispensable part of everyday life, the presence of a strong Scottish industry is likely to have contributed to the ongoing sense of national community and identity, even as Empire and British patriotism reached their zenith. The fact that print culture was relatively autonomous in Scotland effectively helped to structure a separate, but no less rigorous, public sphere within the rest of the United Kingdom. As Brian McNair outlines, the role of a unionist press as a carrier for Scottish national identity was of major significance: 'The voices contributing to that public sphere, and to the periodicals and newspapers which comprised it, believed wholeheartedly in the economic, cultural and political benefits of the union with

England, even if they spoke with a distinctively Scottish voice.' This, argues McNair, would help create 'a print culture recognisably different from that of the London-based press, though rarely conceived of in terms of national separatism.' [189] In the second half of the nineteenth century Scotland experienced a communications revolution which led to the creation of a new popular press owned, written, and distributed within the country that would became a major locus for the imaginative life of the nation.[190] As William Donaldson has shown this development (of which few traces survive today) was spurred on by mass literacy and exemplified by hugely popular publications like the Dundee based *People's Journal*.

Caledonian Importance

With the first stirrings of political Scottish nationalism in the 1920s the basic unionist loyalties of the Scottish press remained concrete. In an era of crisis and conflagration questions such as Home Rule, though fleetingly popular, easily slipped down the political agenda. The scale of economic crisis in Scotland illustrates why: in 1914 the Scottish unemployment rate was below London's, in 1923 it was 125% higher, as Murray Pittock points out: 'Such statistics indicate the contraction of Scotland's position from economic powerhouse of imperial industry to marginal - and increasingly regional - economy. The development of political nationalism against such a background is not surprising, what is perhaps surprising is the length of time it took to make an impact.'[191]

One big outcome for the press in the interwar period was an effort by Canadian-Scot Lord Beaverbrook to make inroads into indigenous Scottish circulations. As the novelist James Barke suggested, this may have indirectly encouraged newspapers in the north to emphasise their small 'n' nationalist credentials: 'The biggest factor contributing to the growth of Scottish Nationalism has its source significantly enough in Fleet Street', wrote Barke in 1932, '…When the race for circulation between the big dailies … was at a crucial stage, they discovered Scotland: the Scots actually bought newspapers,' he added in acerbic mode.[192]

Beaverbrook lavished resources on the *Scottish Daily Express,* of which he was immensely fond, with a 'complete contempt for the canons of profitability.'[193] After the Second World War in a Scotland largely at one with the post-war consensus, newspapers enjoyed a renewed popularity, making the country one of the most competitive newspaper markets anywhere in the world. In the 1960s, the *Daily Record* and the *Scottish Daily Express*, while fiercely competing for each other's readers, boasted a combined circulation of one million.[194] Harry Reid contrasts the status the latter title once enjoyed in Scottish life to its current state, seeing it as 'a pale shadow of the *Scottish Daily Express* in its pomp, a paper that was aggressively Scottish, with a swashbuckling sense of its own Caledonian importance, a Scottish paper that in the 1960s employed over twenty-five feature-writers and over thirty sportswriters.' When the *Express's* Scottish operation collapsed in 1974 due to a breakdown in industrial relations, it was the biggest single blow to the Scottish newspaper industry, with the loss of some 1,800 jobs from its Albion Street offices in Glasgow.[195]

Scotland's print culture is perhaps the unsung hero of the often obscure, but never wholly absent notion of Scotland as a distinct national space. It has been argued, particularly by Karl Deutsch, in his 1966 study, *Nationalism and Social Communication,* that communication is at the heart of the nation, 'Membership in a people essentially consists in wider complementarity of social communications. It consists in the ability to communicate more effectively, and over a wider range of subjects, with members of one large group than with outsiders.'[196] When Benedict Anderson described the development of the nation state alongside standardised vernacular languages he noted, 'the most important thing about language is its capacity for generating imagined communities, building in effect *particular solidarities.'* At the heart of this was the central concept of, 'simultaneity', exemplified in the reading of morning newspapers:

> The significance of this mass ceremony – Hegel observed that newspapers serve modern man as a substitute for morning prayers – is paradoxical. It is performed in silent privacy, in the lair of the skull. Yet each communicant is well aware that the ceremony he performs is being replicated simultaneously by thousands (or millions) of others of whose existence he is confident, yet of whose identity he has not the slightest notion. Furthermore, this ceremony is incessantly repeated at daily or half-daily intervals throughout the calendar. What more vivid figure for the secular, historically clocked, imagined community can be envisioned? [197]

The echoes of Marr's description of the *Scotsman's* journey from its North Bridge fortress, show just how much the production and distribution of a newspaper is, in a sense, a daily nation-making process. Media functions not just as a mass way of disseminating information within a national community. It also plays a deeper, more symbolic role: premised on the act of consumption. Through listening to the radio or reading a newspaper, we subconsciously commune with thousands of other listeners or readers who we will never meet but with whom we share a common experience, primarily via the media channel itself. That no paper on Scotland's breakfast tables ever seriously countenanced the concept of statehood until last year is perhaps more a product of the peculiar, perhaps contradictory, nature of Scottish nationalism. It also owes something to the fact that for generation after generation middle-class readers of broadsheet newspapers were quite comfortable with a vision of a prosperous Scotland, its institutions comfortably nestled into the corners of the union, under which they were often subject to less scrutiny than might have been the case in a more democratic nation. Derek Bateman, who started out as a trainee at the *Scotsman* in the late 1960s, recalls his first day on the job, when it was still closely aligned to the institutions that had governed Scotland for centuries:

> I mean when you came off the train at Waverley and you looked up: it was awesome actually. Genuinely awesome. And I went in to the marble hall of the *Scotsman* with the brass railings on day one and couldn't quite believe I was in there. The *Scotsman* really was something ... You have to remember in those days it was an establishment product in many ways, but it was revered in the way that the banks were revered in the sixties, the church was revered, there was a sense of respect for institutions which has been completely changed in the subsequent period.

The Voice of Civic Scotland

The 1970s and 80s would see the Scottish press adapt to changes in the post-war settlement as it began to be put under increasing strain by a global economic crisis and dramatic political developments. By the 1970s the *Scotsman* expanded its readership significantly under the inspired leadership of Eric Mackay who, building on the solid legacy of his predecessor Alastair Dunnett, turned the paper into a vociferous champion of Home Rule. Journalist George Rosie's claim that 'Eric Mackay did far more than any other journalist to create the Scotland we live in today' is a reminder that, for many, the *Scotsman's* relentless campaigning was the critical factor sustaining the movement to establish a Scottish parliament.[198] As a later *Scotsman* editor, Magnus Linklater, put it, the paper 'once had devolution running through its columns like DNA.' [199] At the same time the paper became a training ground for a cohort of top journalistic talent including Andrew Marr, Neal Ascherson, James Naughtie and Chris Baur. In making an effort to establish itself as the *de facto* national title for Scotland and the key forum for discussion of the nation's constitutional destiny, a quiet, very Scottish civic nationalism became discernible. Partly by design and partly by default, it would come to act as a forum for the expression of civic Scotland's political hopes and aspirations. In a similar process, under the legendary Arnold Kemp, the *Herald* would become a leading advocate of anti-Thatcherism, despite the fact that it had previously cultivated a conservative position. Gerry Hassan sees this as part of a wider process, in which the press would position itself as an opposition to the notorious 'democratic deficit' of this era, 'As the 1980s wore on, the media increasingly donned anti-Thatcher colours, challenged the government and spoke more and more with a nationalist, small 'n' voice, in so doing going with the grain of Scottish society as they had previously done in a different era.'[200] As Maurice Smith recounts in *Paper Lions*, figures in the Conservative Party were so concerned about an anti-Tory consensus in the Scottish press that they considered taking steps to buy out an existing Scottish newspaper or found a new one.[201] With parliamentary politics yet to return to Scotland, in a country ruled by the vast and opaque bureaucracy embodied in St Andrew's House on Calton Hill, papers like the *Scotsman* were to hold up a mirror to Scottish civic life and reflect what it might become if democracy was to return to the north. Iain Macwhirter, is at pains to point out the success of the *Scotsman* in this era:

> The Scotsman was regarded, even by commentators in London, as one of the best produced and most literate

newspapers in the UK. When I was a BBC presenter in Westminster the Scotsman was the only Scottish paper the BBC's parliamentary unit bothered to read, and "The Jock" was almost as influential as the London broadsheets ...This was a publication that spoke confidently to the political elite of the day and expected them to listen.[202]

There are few journalists, who will not speak fondly of what the *Scotsman* once represented. In part, this is the product of nostalgia, but there remains a gap in Scottish public life that no other paper has quite managed to fill. In 1999 Managing Editor Alan Taylor described the particular approach that marked out the paper he oversaw:

I think people understand that the *Scotsman* is the national daily newspaper, but Scotland, no one should underestimate this, is a very tribal country. It's divided into four parts as it were ... and people perceive the *Scotsman* to be an Edinburgh newspaper, the *Scotsman* doesn't perceive itself to be that and it has to take on the role of a national newspaper because none of the other papers want to do that and that brings huge responsibilities with it. You become a newspaper of record, so that you report things straightforwardly, but you invest heavily in things like foreign journalism, international journalism, so that people can see the world from a Scottish perspective, we take that role really, really, seriously.[203]

Such an approach was to be tested in unprecedented ways over the coming years. Taylor's remarks are revealing, not of the status the paper actually enjoyed, but of its desire to compete to be better with the other titles that might one day stake a similar claim. In a

vibrant newspaper market, underpinned with the lucrative advertising revenues that have vanished as surely and inevitably as the
dirty linotype presses themselves, a lot more seemed possible. The
current crisis is demonstrated by the simple fact that no newspaper seems interested in fighting for that prime position as the
paper of record north of the Tweed, respected in London and sure
of its place in relation to wider UK competition. Recent decades
have been disastrous for the Scottish press and having traced their
proud inheritance, we must now look at how that inheritance, so
crucial to the shape and structure of public life in Scotland, risks
being lost for good.

Devolution

There is a certain blindness in Scottish society about how inti-
mately linked politics and media actually are: something that has
become painfully acute since devolution. At the point at which
Scotland most needed a full-scale revival of its print and broadcast media, it entered into a period of precipitous decline. One of
the great ironies about the history of the Scottish press is that the
advent of a Scottish parliament (advocated in its op-ed pages and
leader columns for so long) did not coincide with a revival in the
fortunes of the country's fourth estate. This view was not uniform
and was notoriously challenged by Andrew Neil, editor-in-chief of
Scotsman Publications Limited from 1996-2005. Neil once claimed
that 'devolution was a preoccupation of the Scottish chattering
classes – a body of about 1,000 people – and was not an issue that
the Scottish public really cared about.'[204] The improbable fact that
the arrival of a new centre of political gravity in Edinburgh did
not coincide with a boost to Scotland's papers probably has as
much to do with the nature of devolution itself, as it does with
such lukewarm sentiments. Another factor was a highly successful

response to the new set up from UK titles, with several launching 'tartan editions' and offering products with the heft and range of Fleet Street with additional opinion and reportage from Scotland. In 2009 academic Fiona Douglas pointed to the commercial motives behind such moves, 'Certain UK titles have realised that the Scottish market, with its higher than average appetite for news consumption, was ripe for exploitation.'[205] This was part of a wider process at work in Scotland in the late 1980s and 1990s. Numerous entities, including government bodies, energy companies began to 'Scofity' their brands. With the re-establishment of a parliament in Edinburgh, there was a clear and logical case for the UK press to follow this trend. As former *Sunday Herald* Deputy Editor Joan McAlpine points out, this had something of the reverse effect on the Scottish titles: 'If the kilted London titles had more Scottish content, the indigenous titles increased their non-Scottish material to compete with what readers might consider more sophisticated products. You couldn't be too Scottish, in other words. It was similar to the trend triggered in television by the emphasis on creating content for the network.'[206]

Arnold Kemp, former editor of the *Herald,* summed up the problem, 'It costs much less to 'put a kilt' on a London newspaper with relatively few staff in Scotland than to publish a Scottish newspaper from start to finish.'[207] Had political events in Scotland not taken such a dramatic turn in recent decades, it is perfectly credible that the decline of the Scottish press would, like many such declines in other times and places, have been a quiet process, scarcely noted. Today, the future of the Scottish press in general looks increasingly fragile. The *Scotsman* and its sister titles, purchased for the astonishing sum of £160 million by Johnston Press in December 2005, has been haemorrhaging staff and pagination ever since. Across the board, between 1992 and 2011 circulation of all of Scotland's morning dailies declined drastically: the *Scotsman* was down by 53.9%, the *Herald* by 60.4%, Aberdeen's

Press and Journal by 36.4%, Dundee's *Courier and Advertiser* by 47.9%. Topping the list was the *Daily Record* which saw a fall in its readership of 63.5% over the period.[208] In the case of the *Record*, the arrival of direct red top competition in the form of the *Scottish Sun* (launched in 1987) is a clear demonstration of what direct competition from a far larger UK outfit can do. While such sharp declines in Scottish titles were taking place, sales of English based titles in Scotland rose by 47%. The kind of blanket centralised dominance of the UK media that was not achieved in the nineteenth century seems far more possible in the twenty-first: with the advent of digital media potentially finishing off the job of making metropolitan run media the only game in town. David Hutchison sees this as a stark reversal of the fortunes of indigenous titles, pointing out that (according to his own estimates) they enjoyed a market share of 64% of daily sales and 66% of Sunday titles in the 1970s. Though the Scottish Sunday titles still have a narrow lead over rivals in the south, the Scottish dailies' share of the market is down by around 44%.[209]

Under Andrew Neil's authority – the man the Barclay twins brought in when they purchased the *Scotsman* in 1996 to affect transformation – the paper began to attack its own base. Many have characterised Neil's efforts as representing a campaign against Scotland's centre-left establishment, seen by the right-wing editor as hopelessly statist and unfit for the coming millennium. Though the choice was a controversial one, Neil's reputation was built on turning the *Sunday Times* into the definitive Sunday broadsheet and he had long harboured ambitions to shake up the market in his native land. Throughout this period Neil would lead the paper to make successive decisions that did not naturally chime with its readership, as Stewart Kirkpatrick recalls:

> I didn't view it as a particularly happy time for the paper
> ... Although it was terribly well funded by the Barclays,

they were very generous owners, it lost direction. It went after a kind of 18-30, female, *Daily Mail* reader, without really understanding that that would alienate its existing audience and that the demographic they were trying to reach were already very well served, by the *Daily Mail* ... The *Scotsman* newspaper really abandoned its traditional audience, abandoned what it was, and chased after an audience that was never going to buy the paper. It spent a lot of money doing that, it lost its audience and since then, really, it's never recovered.

The problems that the Scottish press faced were exacerbated by the lack of an engaging political scene developing around the new chamber at Holyrood. As Brian Taylor has argued 'there was a collective view abroad that the press had been corralled for too long into the pro-devolution camp.'[210] With certain exceptions, much of the focus on the early years of devolution was about small-scale scandal, the rigorous journalistic pursuit of which became more easily achieved due to new freedom of information laws. The *Sunday Herald*, founded with a centre-left agenda in the wake of devolution, took a more broad-minded view of proceedings, but was the only significant development in the indigenous press to accompany this historic moment of devolution. In 2000 George Rosie described a state of 'open hostility' between parliamentarians and the Scottish press corps, contrasting it with the formative role it had played in the movement leading to devolution in the preceding decades: 'What pains so many politicians is that, for something like 30 years, the Scottish press – and particularly the *Scotsman* – backed the idea of a Scottish parliament with an enthusiasm that bordered on fanaticism. Now the hacks are sniping, mortaring and shelling their creation to some effect and to the huge distress of its inhabitants.'[211]

Whether less drab administrations in Edinburgh could have

helped revive quality journalism in Scotland at this time or not, is beside the point. The market was becoming crowded and there was little that could have been done to shore up Scottish titles against coming turmoil. There has always been a tendency towards fierce competition for Caledonia's avid readership. Alex Massie clearly defines the problems as one based on a gulf between expectations for higher quality brought about by the concentration of UK titles:

> The quality Scottish newspapers have always been up against it. They have had to fight on three fronts. In the first place they have needed to cover their native heath in exemplary fashion and to a degree none of the London titles can hope to match. But they also need to cover Britain and Westminster effectively since their readers do not consider themselves parochial provincials. And finally, the *Scotsman* (and the *Herald*) were expected to cover the rest of the world, not just because their readers wanted them to but because doing so satisfied their own *amour propre*.[212]

In other words, the relative sophistication and attractiveness of the Scottish newspaper market, which as recently as 2009 boasted levels of consumption that were 10% higher than the rest of the country, played a part in its downfall.[213] Yet only a decade ago it seemed that the quality Scottish press was in decent health, not least because companies like Johnston Press and Newsquest were handing over vast sums for a share of the action. Newsquest paid £216m for the *Herald*, the *Sunday Herald* and the *Evening Times* in 2004.

Survivors

'They did not care about producing quality at all. They only cared about producing profit. We all came back with our heads hung low and feeling very miserable about the whole business and it just went from bad to worse.' This was former *Scotsman* editor John McGurk's assessment of Johnston Press's purchase of the *Scotsman* titles in 2005.[214] No single factor has resulted in the undead picture of Scottish press than the totemic mistake of viewing newspapers like the *Scotsman* as inherently profitable assets that guaranteed a return on investment envied by other sectors. Post crash, an industry crippled by ownership structures from a different economic era is fighting for survival. This is hugely problematic for the entire sector, as Phillip Meyer has pointed out, 'there is no easy way to get from a newspaper industry used to 20 to 40 percent margins to one that is content with 6 or 7. The present owners have those margins built into their expected return on investment, which is related to their standard of living.'[215]

After the financial collapse of 2008, newspaper staff find themselves caught in a suffocating trap: working on titles that were bought up by large companies, like Johnston Press, in the good times, when they seemed destined to always generate a profit. Few could have foreseen the financial collapse, or how toxic the combination of that event with the shift of revenue online would be. Peter Geoghegan, a freelance journalist based in Scotland, describes the meagre inheritance left to today's press:

> Both the *Herald* and the *Scotsman* were bought by media groups with ideas above their station during a boom. Unfortunately for the newspaper industry, booms have happened throughout capitalism ... But the difference with this boom was that the bust that followed it was coterminous with the development of mobile apps and

digital platforms and the fact that the people were now able to consume media without buying newspapers, so when the bust hit, and it hit newspapers bad, we're not able to go back again.

In February 2015 McGurk noted, 'the time is surely approaching when the *Scotsman*, as a printed newspaper, is no longer viable or sustainable. Producing it online only would eliminate newsprint, production and distribution costs in one fell swoop and, hopefully, allow some of these savings to be ploughed into making scotsman. com.'[216] His comments were based on figures that suggested an average of only 16,887 full price copies of the paper were sold on a daily basis. The prospect of the end of one Scottish national paper is now more real than ever. 'Johnston Press, more than any other,' wrote Arthur MacMillan in 2012, 'is the British newspaper company that ate itself.' By borrowing heavily to cover a series of buy-outs in this period, the company, the second largest publisher of local newspapers in the UK, was entirely unprepared for the turbulent times ahead. Since then, massive falls in circulation and advertising revenue have seen staffing decimated. According to the company's own figures, across its titles, 635 journalists have been lost, while MacMillan claims the number of staff employed at the *Scotsman* had halved by 2008 and has continued to decline since. It has also seen a fall of around 80% in its readership since 2006. As one executive at the title recalled just after the acquisition, 'It was apparent to me, almost instantly, that they did not know what they had bought and were completely out of their depth.'[217] McGurk's final assessment of the paper's current plight doesn't pull any punches:

The *Scotsman* no longer makes money; the presses in Edinburgh have been sold off; the staff have been moved out of the Holyrood building into a 1960s office block towards the outskirts of the city and, appropriately, across the road from a cemetery. The harsh reality is that lack of resource and precious few editorial staff makes it hugely difficult to produce a newspaper which stands out from the other 16 daily newspapers on sale in Scotland. Too many front pages are a summary of the previous night's television news, a formula for further readership decline.

For Stewart Kirkpatrick, the story is one of major mismanagement of a paper staffed by, 'people who probably are more committed to the product than the company that owns the product.' Those working at the paper find themselves in a cruel cycle, knowing that the resources required to produce a quality paper are simply not forthcoming:

> The *Scotsman* is produced by a very small number of journalists who are worked far too hard, the paper is direc- tionless, the quality of the content isn't very good and that isn't a reflection on the abilities of the people who work there. I know most of the people who work there, they are committed and they are talented people but they are being given an impossible mission, which is to try and produce a high quality product with tiny resources and also without a real sense of what the *Scotsman* is for. It looks to me like a newspaper that is brought out by the skin of its teeth, by a small desperate band of survivors.

This era of vast constitutional questions and intense political battles is one in which it has become increasingly difficult to work as a journalist in Scotland. Yet never has Scotland had a greater need for quality journalism, to help it understand the rapid changes that have taken place in its politics and wider society than today. The relative health of the Dundee and Aberdeen titles owned by

DC Thomson could offer a model for revival (the *Press and Journal* now boasts a circulation greater than the *Herald* and the *Scotsman* combined)[218] but the company has shown little interest in moving either title into the 'national' Scottish market, and its notoriously secretive, conservative practices may not be geared towards innovation. The *Sunday Herald*, bucking the trend and increasing its sales as the only paper to back independence during the referendum, is of course an exception to this picture. Yet, overall, as Hutchison has pointed out, all of these rapid developments may perversely spell the end of national newspapers in Scotland: 'The media, which should be the lifeblood of the debate, are losing readers, journalists and standing. Indigenous newspapers are shrinking, staff are being cut and, at a time when information and informed opinion should be at a premium, the means by which they are conveyed are being squeezed to the point of extinction.'[219]

Conclusion

> The first duty of the Press is to obtain the earliest and most correct intelligence of the events of the time, and instantly by disclosing them, to make them the common property of the nation.
>
> John Thadeus Delane (1817-79)[220]

In a remarkably prescient lecture in 1996, one of the most respected Scottish journalists of the twentieth century, Arnold Kemp, foresaw the current plight of the Scottish press. Kemp, who had edited the *Herald* for 14 years, perceived the challenges presented by digital technology and the already noticeable impact of the 'tartan editions'. He posed a question that is still essentially unanswered. Referring to the national Scottish dailies, he pointed out that they were faced with a choice, to either become local or to remain national, but, he warned:

> The national role is more ambitious and much more difficult. It implies greater editorial resources to justify a premium price. It means having the capital resources to develop, perhaps in the electronic media, new revenue sources to replace the old. It is the more demanding option – but it is the only one worth having. If we do not fight to preserve it, then the bleak conclusion for any serious Scottish journalist who wants to deal with the central policy issues of his time will be that he cannot do this in his own country. [221]

Kemp, who worked at both the *Scotsman* and the *Herald*, saw rivalry between the two papers as the dynamic that underpinned quality journalism north of the border. 'Competition within Scotland between the *Herald* and the *Scotsman* is crucial to the health of our Scottish national press because it forces proprietors to release resources … Yet unless its revenues are sustained, a serious Scottish press cannot exist,' he said, adding with a sombre note, 'The commercial pressure on newspapers to maximize the returns of the business have increased to an intensity which may not always be compatible with the public interest.'[222]

This is perhaps why, welcome though another daily newspaper must always be, the *National*, with its tiny staff, can only do so much to address the decline of Scotland's newspaper market. It also cannot, by definition, compete with its ancient sister, as can be clearly seen in its content. Post-referendum, given that intense phase of almost uniform messages promoted by the Scottish press, it is deeply troubling that a once vibrant fourth estate could so singularly militate against a view that was eventually expressed by 1.6 million Scots. It did not have to be this way. In fact until relatively recently it was possible to see the Scottish press playing an active role in the development of the independence cause. As journalist and presenter Magnus Magnusson suggested in 2006:

> I believe that, when we get independence, a lot of it will be due to the way in which the Scottish press has not let the idea slip out of the public mind. That is, the constant reminders of what devolution is about, what the national identity is about, what independence is about. In twenty years time, I expect to see an independent Scottish nation. Much of the credit for that will go to the Scottish press.[223]

On the far side of 18 September 2014, the Scottish press has sacrificed much of its credibility and influence, not on the altar of Scottish statehood, but in an effort to preserve union. The historic tone of Scottish newspapers, which saw the country first and foremost as an interesting, distinct place, and shaped its offering accordingly, now seems scarce where it ought to be abundant. The market in Scotland is failing and whether or not a revived Scottish journalism would, perhaps through the sheer force of its nerve, boost the Scottish independence cause, is far from clear. We can however assert that newspapers did play a significant role in forming opinions during the referendum, despite all of the issue listed above. YouGov found that 60% of us relied on print or digital versions of Scottish newspapers to inform opinion on the debate. While this figure was outstripped by television and radio at 71% the role of newspapers in setting the agendas of broadcasters, particularly for the BBC, remains significant.[224]

So the press still plays a vital role as a steward of the information that makes democracy possible in Scotland. There is no shortage of veteran Scottish journalists and editors who have pondered darkly on the arrival of a doomsday moment for the newspaper in Scotland. Like Ian Jack, many see the possibility as both entirely credible and yet also unimaginable, 'Nothing in Scotland's history suggests that it would abandon its newspapers so readily, or at a time when reading a good one might be more necessary.'[225] Fiona Douglas, an academic, sums up the tenor of them all when stating 'The consequence of a devolved or even independent Scotland without its own national press to speak for it and scrutinise it are unthinkable.'[226] As Magnus Linklater said of the *Scotsman's* referendum predicament, 'At this critical point, for which its whole history should have been a preparation, it is shorn of pages and profile.'[227]

The case for a Scottish media is founded on a rich historic heritage, on the sense that, if the decline of the press was to follow through to actual demise, something irreplaceable would be lost to Scottish society. It would mean the ultimate end of a solid tradition, of a rivalry founded on holding power to account and strengthening the quality of the national conversation. The *Scotsman* in its prime, as described by Alan Taylor is compelling, 'Its thistle-bedecked masthead evoked gravitas and authority and a prickly sense of place. It was Scotland's voice in the world...'[228] This is precisely what is lost when papers opt for Kemp's 'local' strategy. We risk losing the ability to talk to each other and to better comprehend our place in the world. At a time when Scotland's relationship with the rest of the UK and Europe is becoming increasingly contested, a task that should be paramount has instead become an obscure pursuit. With a quiet, but nonetheless authentic note of tragedy, the Scottish press has lost, along with its readership, a sense of what it is for.

This is why, as we have seen through looking at the historic role and specific structure of the public sphere in Scotland, a diverse press liberated from the immediate crises of commercial failure, is fundamental to the entire concept of Scotland as a nation, as an imagined community. Borrowing another line from Anderson gives a better picture of what is at stake: 'Communities are to be distinguished' he writes, 'not by their falsity/genuineness, but by the style in which they are imagined.'[229] It is in no small part through the daily commerce of words and ideas, embodied by newspapers and journalism, that this process takes place. There is no 'genuine' or 'false' nation to aspire to, there is only the communicative space, through which a nation is constituted. We need both stylistically bold, rigorous, quality journalism in all its forms, offering choice that is reflective of the diverse and multiform Scotland that is so often reduced to being either one thing or the other. While the notion of an independent Scottish press does not necessarily mean an independent Scotland, it does mean that the civic life of the nation will stand a chance of survival in a constantly shifting world. As Craig Calhoun reminds us, '… A public sphere adequate to a democratic polity depends upon both quality of discourse and quantity of participation.'[230]

Nations have come and gone with the capacity to realise their imagined solidarity in print. If, as Ernest Renan remarked, the nation is a kind of daily plebiscite, we need that daily connection to the wider polity for it to function. Renan also pointed out that, 'Forgetting, I would even go so far as to say historical error, is a crucial factor in the creation of a nation.'[231] It may well be that in Scotland's long and complex struggle to situate its own nation-status within the broader scheme of things, that the contribution of its press to that process will be placed to one side. This would be, on balance, a great loss that would cut across the contours of whatever political divides might be abroad in the country if such a day were to come. For there is a respected, at points even a radical, heritage that Scottish journalism, with its typically gruff, self-deprecating manner is often incapable of articulating. It is indeed poignant that one of the best assertions of why an atrophied press is simply not good enough, was made in the *Scotsman's* opening pitch when it launched in 1817, 'Many political transactions are never generally known, and the conductors of the Edinburgh prints act editorially as if they dreaded nothing so much as the idea of being thought independent. Contrasted with the London, or many even of the provincial newspapers, those of Edinburgh are cold, unvaried and spiritless'. [232] If modern Scotland can thole a press that so often seems cold, unvaried and spiritless, or for that matter a country in which politics is an aloof matter for those who know best, then we should abandon any notion of refashioning the public sphere in Scotland. If, however, we want something better, there remains a persuasive, broad and civic case for a systematic revival of Scottish journalism.

6

Spaces of Autonomy

It began on the Internet social networks, as these are spaces of autonomy, largely beyond the control of governments and corporations that had monopolised the channels of communication as the foundation of their power, throughout history. By sharing sorrow and hope in the free public space of the Internet, by connecting to each other, and by envisioning projects from multiple sources of being, individuals formed networks, regardless of their personal views or organizational attachments. They came together. And their togetherness helped them to overcome fear, the paralyzing emotion on which the powers that be rely in order to prosper and reproduce, by intimidation and discouragement.

Manuel Castells, *Networks of Outrage and Hope*[233]

On 19 September 2014 something remarkable happened. It was not, in and of itself, newsworthy. But it demonstrated succinctly just how much Scotland had changed in the preceding months and years. The referendum result had seen many hopes dashed. The numbers were stark for the Yes campaign, the result was closer than expected, but still decisive enough to afford the No camp the comfort of a clear victory. Scotland voted against the Scottish Government entering into negotiations to end the country's three hundred year old union. Glasgow, North Lanarkshire, Dundee and West Dunbartonshire voted Yes, while areas such as Dumfries and Galloway, Edinburgh, the Scottish Borders and Orkney returned No votes in excess of 60%. Yet even as defeat began to look inevitable people came together online.

If social media's legendary ability to magnify grassroots political organising was not enough to win the referendum for Yes, it undoubtedly played a pivotal role in shaping how pro-independence activists coped with its loss. As Scotland woke up on a definitively dreich morning that September, a vast process of regrouping, mutual grieving, reassurance and inspiration was already underway. The power of the network made itself felt. In the week leading up to the vote a sense of euphoria had gripped swathes of the country, passions ran high on the streets, with an openness and fervency rarely seen in an often tongue-tied society. Crowds made up of families, students, hardened activists, and pensioners took to the street in spontaneous gatherings planned on social media. The most symbolic of these, in Glasgow's George Square, provided the most iconic images of the referendum. These events were overwhelmingly peaceful. Over the course of several days not a single arrest was made. The only victim was the Corrie's 'Flower of Scotland': the nation's sporting anthem murdered by hoarse vocal chords for hours on end. The dark inversion of those images, now imprinted on Scotland's collective memory, began to take shape on the evening of Friday 19 September. Loyalist groups, led by Britain First, arrived to 'take back' George Square. Eleven arrests were made and by the evening violence was seen throughout the city centre.[234] Given that the story of Scotland's referendum had officially closed, the initial response to these events from news organisations was slow, live pictures were hard to come by, with the BBC framing the event as a clash of 'rival groups.' In a moment of fear and confusion, Scotland's media deficit seemed immediate and suffocating. With limited access to live pictures of the scene, word was largely spread via Twitter, with pro-independence activists warning each other to steer clear of the area or to help document the violence and intimidation. That such a dramatic and newsworthy event would not meet with a rapid response right across the media seemed remarkable. When contrasted with the almost obsessive coverage of even the slightest scuffle on the campaign trail and pre-Poll warnings about 'carnage' detailed above, the muted response seemed hypocritical. But these events did not fit with any pre-existing narrative or establishment view. In fact, they clashed with extensive press coverage that painted *Scottish* nationalism as thuggish and intimidating. This was despite the fact that, as Peter Geoghegan later reflected, senior unionists had encouraged displays of British identity:

> Political leaders were encouraging Scots to fly the Union flag and have pride in Britain's imperial past. As Scotland went to the polls, an image of Britannia circulated online, depicting Alex Salmond's severed head skewered on her trident. Scotland's much heralded democratic renewal cuts both ways: in the view of many Loyalists, the referendum result is a vindication of their deeply sectarian worldview.[235]

This was a rare case, in a western democracy, of citizen journalism actually proving necessary to document events to cover what was taking place on the ground. As *Wings Over Scotland's* Stuart Campbell explained, this was felt to be a definitive breach of trust, not least because many Scots had to piece together fragments of information, off their own back, about an alarming situation:

> We watched it on live video feeds from the state broadcasters of other countries, ones we've been taught to

regard as less truthful than our own. We saw it on pictures and Vines and video clips sent by people who were actually there ... But we don't know about it from the BBC. The BBC's story was for many hours tucked away halfway down a piece about Alex Salmond resigning. Eventually it got a page of its own where it was portrayed as a clash between rival groups, rather than what it was – a mob of thugs attacking people who'd been peacefully and happily assembled in the square for days, with not a single disturbance or arrest.[236]

These twin experiences immediately after the referendum – of fear, confusion, disconnect on the one hand and mass regrouping on the other – had a profound impact. At stake for those who advocated change in 2014 was a repeat of that sudden loss of purpose amongst those who had campaigned for devolution, and failed (albeit due to a technicality) to win in 1979. Of the many Scots who saw a moment to leave Scotland, the intellectual stalwart of the *Scotsman* for some years, Neal Ascherson, was among the most prominent. Ascherson's reflection on the difference before and after the outcome is recalled with a visceral intensity in his memoir *Stone Voices:*

During those years, they had grown accustomed to the idea that Scotland was to become an exciting, lively little country in which their talents would be needed. In the diary, I wrote: 'The future existed for many years; people became used to it as a background; now it has vanished and there is a blankness only.' People seemed to shrink and fade. Many turned to alcohol, some to hard drugs. Many more fell back into the old assumption that Scotland was a dead-end ('there's nothing for young folk here'), and they left for London, America or continental Europe. The failure of self-government ruined many lives, and they were not the lives of politicians.[237]

Of course there are vast differences between 1979 and 2014. Political alignments, economic circumstances, the issues at stake and the nature of the campaigns are all strikingly dissimilar. By 2014 an authentically Scottish politics had taken root via devolution, focused on a parliament with far greater powers than those promised in the event of a Yes vote in 1979. However, the stakes in Scotland's most recent referendum were noticeably higher, as was the level of public emotion. This made it all the more surprising when it became clear that a No vote did not, as many had assumed, hole the SNP below the waterline. The broad church movement that had gathered behind Yes did not evaporate. Remarkably, the opposite occurred. As Ascherson himself noted of the result shortly after 18 September 2014, 'The sense of onrush, of irresistible change, has survived the 'No' vote. For a party in defeat to double its membership in five days – that sort of thing just doesn't happen in Britain.'[238] It would be too simplistic to attribute the astonishingly rapid growth in the membership of pro-independence parties to social media alone, but it played a pivotal role in fuelling that continued sense of movement. While the lion's share of new recruits went to the SNP, big surges were also seen in the ranks of the Scottish Green Party and the Scottish Socialist Party. Many decided to group themselves under the banner 'the #45' literally wearing the badge of defeat with collective pride. There was an immediate urge across a range of fields to do *something*. In many cases, this involved small acts like donating to a food bank, for others the next phase of the movement was already being planned. Some of the reactions were slightly premature and ill thought out, including a raft of theories as to how the vote had been rigged and several groups attempting to raise funds to start television news services. But overall the response was to strengthen existing groups, not just the parties, but non-aligned campaigns like Common Weal and Women for Independence too.

A Networked Social Movement

2011 is still remembered as the year that showcased what unfettered access to digital platforms could do to assist grassroots activism, particularly during the Arab Spring. Social media, regardless of where it gets used, seems to inevitably bring with it a lot of hype. But there is a rational case for the power of networks too. Writing in the wake of the Arab Spring and the phone hacking scandal, Paul Mason was emphatic about the significance of these new ways of organising:

> The network, in short, has begun to erode power relation-ships we had come to believe were permanent features of capitalism: the helplessness of the consumer, the military-style hierarchy of boss and underlings at work, the power of mainstream media empires to shape ideology, the repressive capabilities of the state and the inevitability of monopolization by large corporations.[239]

Whatever its faults, during the referendum a sense of alien-ation from the mainstream created a strong online sub-culture, a network of hope. Though vilified by newspapers like the *Daily Mail* as a breeding ground for abusive internet trolls or 'cybernats', it did in fact contain a whole raft of activity: from documentary film making, crowd funding, blogging, art, satire, memes, and highly visible online advances in the broader campaign (hashtags instigated by arts-based campaign group National Collective for example trended globally). Perhaps most importantly, these online networks provided a space that allowed an alternative to mainstream media narratives to be put forward. They also offered the opportunity for specific assertions by politicians, broadcasters and newspapers to be contested, debunked and constantly scrutinised. Though it is impossible to quantify the agency that new media provided within the context of the referendum campaign, it is worth considering how different things might have been had the referendum taken place twenty years earlier, prior to its development. If nothing else, it's likely that many of the highly questionable editorial decisions taken by the mainstream media would simply not have been challenged.

Speaking to the *Drum* in 2014 *Sunday Herald* and *National* editor Richard Walker observed how well alternative media had filled the gap by meeting the demand for pro-independence voices, 'Because of what I'd describe as a democratic deficit, because there have not been newspapers in the mainstream media which support independence then there's a vacuum there and websites such as *Bella Caledonia* and *Wings Over Scotland* have stepped into that vacuum.'[240] There are numerous factors behind the massive political changes that Scotland has experienced in recent years but it does seem likely that its arrival served to 'tool up' supporters of change, while amplifying a wider sense of empowerment, voice and agency. The movement fitted with Castells' concept of the 'networked social movement' using the autonomy available online as a means to circumvent an old hierarchical structure (in this case the British political establishment). As Mike Small, Editor of *Bella Caledonia* noted in the early stages of the referendum campaign:

It's well documented how the photocopier contributed to the downfall of the Soviet Union. During the Yugoslav Wars in the 1990s, B92 was one of the very few sources for news not controlled by Milošević regime – it became an exemplar of a free media – a touchstone for a younger generation. Radio and now online radio are difficult to

shut down. Each shifting tide of social change drives and
is driven by new forms. The disintegration of the British
state is no different, and the wider reactionary forces that
Rothermere, Murdoch, and Desmond represent will not be
missed with their explicit agenda of bigotry and conservatism.[241]

Digital and social media have served to radically devolve
publishing power and there can be little doubt that globally new
media has played an important role in disseminating alternative
views. As part of the campaign, the explosion of new media in
Scotland played a key role in mobilising and organising the pro-
independence camp. Yes Scotland Chief Executive Blair Jenkins
saw this as a key element to the campaign he oversaw, 'the two
areas where we thought we could win and where I think we did
win were in face to face campaigning and in social media. We set
out very deliberately from the beginning to be strong in those two
areas.' This picture was backed up by external sources, including
Conor Magowan, Director of Public Affairs for Scotland at Weber
Shandwick, who told the *Financial Times* two days before the vote,
'The digital generation looks more inclined to vote Yes.' Such
comments would seem to align with findings from the extensive
Scottish Referendum Study which found significant generational
gaps behind the headline results, with younger voters registering
majorities for Yes.[242]

But the networks that connected the Yes movement were some
time in the making. One of the key difference that will define the
coming shape of Scotland's new media landscape is whether this
great opening up of online activity will serve as an arm of the wider
movement for independence, or seek to go beyond the political
ties that gave birth to it. Looking at the new media platforms that
have emerged in Scotland, it's not yet clear yet if such leaps can
be made, or if this vast ephemera generating machine can actually

organise and turn itself into a kind of alternative media service.

When Joan McAlpine proclaimed in a *Sunday Times* column in December 2009 that 'Cybernats are the new Pamphleteers' the blogosphere that she described was based largely on individuals. Contrasting it with the established Northern Irish site *Slugger O'Toole*, which hosts of a range of opinion, she pointed out, 'Scotland is different in that our bloggers are highly individualised.' Early examples of forays into political blogging in Scotland were indeed largely individual efforts including, *Scot Goes Pop* (James Kelly) *Lallands Peat Worrier* (Andrew Tickell), *Moridura* (Peter Curran) *Thoughtland* (Pat Kane) and Mike Small and Kevin Williamson's *Bella Caledonia,* which first appeared in November 2007. The first attempt at a comprehensive 'news and views' site came with the launch of *Newsnet Scotland* in March 2010. *Better Nation,* setting out to offer a mix of views, launched in September 2010. One of its founders, James Mackenzie, contrasts Scotland's online commentariat at the start of the decade with its current state, 'To be quite honest, I think the blogging scene was more diverse then and more interesting. It was also more social, with semi-regular meetups and idea-sharing. With a very few exceptions - *Peat Worrier* being the most notable - it feels pretty dead now, and *Better Nation's* dormant state is a symptom of that.' It was, ironically, a disagreement over comments on the latter site with a guest blogger, one Stuart Campbell, that led to the most notable success story of Scottish online media. *Wings Over Scotland* was founded in 2011, six months after the Scottish Parliament elections of that year. 'I was blocked from commenting on my own article,' says Campbell, 'I'd written them a piece (on why the SNP should stand in England) and was debating it perfectly civilly with some readers when I found myself summarily blocked without warning because I'd made what was deemed by *BN* to be a politically-incorrect remark about the Welsh language.'

Mackenzie disputes this and regrets the more combative,

aggressive tone taken by blogs like *Wings*, 'I would like to think there's a space for more cross-party and non-party blogging, something which reflects an understanding that even when we disagree it's often for good and honest reasons, rather than an idea that "they" are "the enemy", determined to destroy Scotland by backing the wrong constitutional option.' Controversies aside, the success of Wings has been the subject of a great deal of speculation, smears and envy within the ranks of the traditional media. In February 2015 the *Daily Record* described the site as 'fuelling a world of conspiracy theories, hatred and paranoia.'[243] The site's notoriety in certain quarters is perhaps due to the remarkable scale of its success: by April 2015 *Wings* was being visited by 366,201 unique users, and a poll conducted by Panelbase ranked it at number 3, after BBC and STV, as the website that respondents visited 'at least once a week specifically for political content.'[244] On top of its popularity, *Wings* has shown a remarkable ability to finance itself through crowdfunding. In 2013 the site managed to raise £30,000, in 2014 another campaign raised over £90,000 and by March 2015 a third crowdfunder had pulled in upwards of £110,000. For Campbell there is no obvious reason behind this rare ability to make online journalism pay, 'why we have such incredible success with fundraising while others struggle is a question I'm not really equipped to answer,' he says, adding, 'If I had to hazard a guess I'd say it's at least partly about striking a balance between serious, evidence-based analysis and quick, snarky funny stuff that helps keep people's spirits up. Being "worthy" is all very well, but all writing is also about entertainment on some level, and you have to make people *want* to read stuff, not just feel that they *ought* to.'

The ability of individual sites like *Wings* to build up a community of readers and supporters shows just how far new media in Scotland has moved from its somewhat wonkish origins. Sites like *Wings* have been complimented by the beginnings of a wider media ecology now taking shape online. *The Ferret*, a collective of freelance investigative journalists launched in 2015, crowdfunds investigations to pursue the aim of 'nosing up the trouser leg of power'. The site has the potential to offer an often elusive and time consuming form of journalism a much needed platform in Scotland. As co-founder Rob Edwards remarked it seeks to redress this systemic problem: 'We did this because, looking forward, it was hard for us to see how good, fact-based, non-aligned investigative journalism would be funded.'[245] In the wake of the referendum Common Weal launched *Common Space,* employing an editor and three part time journalists, the first staffed website in Scotland to focus on news gathering rather than opinion. *Newsnet Scotland* has adopted a hybrid mix of opinion led content and broadcast interviews overseen by BBC veterans Maurice Smith and Derek Bateman. *Bella Caledonia* now employs a full time editor and has won a reputation for itself as the pre-eminent home of online pro-independence think pieces. Podcasts such as *NewsShaft* and *aPolitical* offer weekly alternative politics coverage, though *Newsshaft* has since closed due to financial pressures after attempting to professionalise and expand its remit. Vlogger Stephen Paton's *Left Scotland* offers a 'resource for activists' and videos on different themes, in addition to regular instalments. Independence Live have a remarkable presence on the ground, live streaming political meetings and protests from locations all over the country. Other blogs offer radical perspectives grounded in activism: the queer-feminist blog *A Thousand Flowers* packs an irreverent, wit-laden and subversive punch. The Green oriented *Post* has pioneered a model of a Creative Commons focused media collective, with several print offerings emerging since it launched in 2013.

Citizen Witnessing

The big question that emerges from all of this activity is whether it can sustain itself in the longer term. Vast amounts of this media content is created on a voluntary basis. While its heyday during the referendum was a definitive part of envisioning a new Scotland, creating activist media is a far more open and accessible task than hard journalism – with its inherent need for building professional contacts, long hours, fact checking and other laborious, intensive practices. The concept of 'citizen journalism' first came to prominence during the 2004 Indian Ocean tsunami, when the effects of the disaster caused news organisations to become almost entirely dependent on footage that had been gathered and sent in by viewers on the ground.[246] Increasingly, desk bound staff journalists often find that aggregating an array of content gathered on smartphones by members of the public can add colour and vibrancy to a tough news day. The irony of the reliance of 'old media' on external sources is highlighted by Nick Davies, 'Huge organisations whose sole purpose in life is to gather news are too busy with their churnalism to find out what is happening.'[247] In that sense, 'citizen journalism' is actually performing the task of content creation for old fashioned news organisations to sift through and make use of, 'It is cheap labour,' says academic Tamara Witschgeon on *openDemocracy*, 'outsourcing salaried work to amateurs ... to the benefit of the large profit-making multinationals.'[248] The real breakthrough moment for 'citizen journalism' was, tellingly, an accident. Sohaib Attar, a Pakistani who live-tweeted the raid on Osama Bin Laden's compound as it took place not far from his desk in Abbottabad, broke the story before news organisations were aware that it had occurred. The capacity of anyone with a broadband or 3G connection to publish and document what is happening in their locality is an exceptionally powerful force. It can, in certain circumstances, throw massively powerful, hierarchical organisations off kilter.

The Athar case has become increasingly normalised, those who are transfixed by watching events unfold increasingly look to Twitter as a source for primary information and live updates. This version of citizen journalism is better described, as in Stuart Allan's study, as *Citizen Witnessing*. In part this is because, as Allan argues, there is something fundamental about the professional duty to tell the story that cannot be embodied in every citizen. Then again, the act of 'witnessing' itself is being put under increasing strain, often by the application of draconian laws designed to apply to publishers being transferred to individuals with social media accounts. As a result, journalism has become, in Allan's words, 'A site of struggle over one of the most vital of human rights, the right to bear witness.'[249]

Cognitive Surplus

Whether all of this activity in Scotland can equate to an alternative platform for journalism, on a scale to rival the old commercial model, remains to be seen. It is also unclear whether journalism as a clearly defined profession that produces discrete products is sustainable in the longer term. In an era defined by what Axel Burns has called 'produsage', namely, 'The collaborative and continuos building and extending of existing content in pursuit of further improvement' it seems increasingly at odds with wider changes in society. Burns describes produsage and how it contrasts with the traditional distinction between producers and consumers:

>...especially where what is produced is of an intangible, informational nature, a further shift away from such industrial, and towards postindustrial or informational economic models can be observed. In such models, the production of ideas takes place in a collaborative, partici-

patory environment which breaks down the boundaries between producers and consumers and instead enables all participants to be users as well as producers of information and knowledge – frequently in an inherently and inextricably hybrid role where usage is necessarily also productive.[250]

Media, in some sense, has always mirrored the prevailing mode of production in a given society. Today, our need to organise time in a fixed and regimented way in order to match fixed work patterns is eroding. There's an argument that the distinction between our leisure time, once defined by habits like fag and tea breaks and clearly differentiated zones of work and play, is starting to fade. Smartphones have replaced smoking as the default way to frame time and book end social situations.[251] But the nature of our leisure time has also become radically altered by the power of the internet. Clay Shrikey,'s idea of *Cognitive Surplus*, suggests that our ability to form connections allows us to turn our free time into a socially useful, productive tool on an unprecedented scale:

More value can be gotten out of voluntary participation than anyone previously imagined, thanks to improvements in our ability to connect with one another and improvements in our imagination of what is possible from such participation. We are emerging from an era of theory-induced blindness in which we thought sharing (and most non market interactions) was inherently rather than accidentally limited to small, tight-knit groups.[252]

The point here is not that we all do for free roles that were previously paid for. Rather, it is that numerous small acts, sharing, liking, re-tweeting, commenting, donating, when wired up to the massive aggregative power of the internet, can generate immensely powerful results. For now, the fixed by-line and the status of a single author remains a deeply embedded part of what journalism is. But perhaps journalism, or the shape of the media product itself will become increasingly collaborative. To an extent this is already the case, clearly a big part of the success of a website like *Wings Over Scotland* is the active, discursive community that is drawn to it. Part of the experience offered is a communal one, in that sense it is more akin to chat rooms and forums that characterised the early days of the web. Certainly, online spaces are far more open to submissions from users and of course many are also able to interact with each other's views through the still extant, if less prominent blogosphere. Essentially many of these initiatives are framed, at least in a rhetorical manner, as collective efforts. The need to crowdfund not only fixes the Scottish alternative media into a kind of constant campaigning and movement-sustaining mode, but it also builds a far closer relationship with its audience than would ever have been possible in an old media setting. This kind of openness and accountability means that acts of support, sharing, commenting and distribution can create the sense of a shared project. This is why sites that have offered a clearly defined product, with very little in the way of management speak or hype, such as *Wings Over Scotland,* have often been the most successful. The 'consumers' feel part of the action too. 'It's something that just seems to happen organically if you write a certain way. Treat readers with respect – by making your arguments clearly and candidly and backing them up with evidence – and they'll tend to respond in kind,' says Campbell. He also maintains that having to resort to advertising rather than crowd funding would probably spell the end of the venture: 'I'd really hate to be ad-funded … If crowdfunding ever dries up for Wings, I don't know if I'd even try to continue it with ads. It's a fundamentally ethically and professionally bad basis for journalism.'

The self-generating movement that emerged in 2014 was partly the result of the steady hollowing out and eventual collapse of Labour Scotland. The Party had for generations represented the nationalised, Fordist model of production, of primarily male workers on assembly lines and in heavy industries. Labour spoke for those people, for years ensuring they were paid a decent wage and had a roof over their head. As the nationalised industries disappeared and the housing was neglected or sold off, a new political force was always bound to challenge it. That force was younger, infinitely less corrupt and had technology on its side. But now that we live in a world of software, collaboration, produsage and mass smartphone use, there is an expectation to participate rather than to merely follow. These new lifestyles, which are often less fixed in terms of vocation and identity, are infinitely more precarious, but are often far more creative and selective. Production is now often 'immaterial' and is likely to become increasingly so as automation becomes ever more pervasive. The old class distinctions of broadsheet and tabloid must surely begin to lose their grip as the social pressure to select one or another wanes. The way that papers are produced though, the 'daily' aspect, is still one of the most powerful pulls of traditional media (which is, if anything increased in the less strictly clocked post-Fordist world) but this is essentially a technical matter. That inherent ability to constantly revise digital media is crucial: information is no longer trapped in a fixed form as it once was. Perhaps the biggest alteration will be in the idea of regular fixed 'editions', with Wikipedia as a pre-eminent case in point for how collaboration can completely alter how we value ideas like authorship and discrete versions of a product. As Burns points out, '...Journalism's industrial production practices are better suited to a traditional model providing for news updates at regularly scheduled times than for a 24-hour production cycle, for example.' [253]

The model that media corporations have long operated under is only partly premised on the selling of a media product to a specific audience. Of far more importance is the selling of access to that audience to advertisers. As Jean Seaton and James Curran have argued, advertisers inevitably shape the space and agenda of the platforms that they chose to access consumers through.[254] To an extent this system of funding journalism was always bound to lack stability. For Raymond Williams advertising is a 'magic system' closely associated with the monopoly capitalism that emerged around the turn of the last century:

> If the consumption of individual goods leaves that whole area of human need unsatisfied, the attempt is made, by magic, to associate this consumption with human desires to which it has a real reference. You do not only buy an object: you buy social respect, discrimination, health, beauty, success, power to control your environment. The magic obscures the real source of general satisfaction because their discovery would involve radical change in the whole common way of life.[255]

As consumer needs are met with increasing accuracy via search engines and the capture of online data, the kind of 'magic' system for creating new desires that Williams describes is rendered obsolete. The relationship between journalism and its source of revenue is always controversial and the current mix of commercial interests, large multinationals who have largely monopolised online revenue does not seem to offer much in the way of comfort.

Can the new media revolution be crowdfunded? Can we simply look to Twitter and online networks for that constantly evolving, adapting and (hopefully) improving media product? Or have we forgotten one of the most basic tenets that this book started out with, the ability of journalists: 'the professional storytellers of our age' to travel, to translate, to interrogate and to contextualise on our behalf? To go where readers, for whatever reason, cannot. There is no escaping the fact that, whatever its form or delivery mechanism, if we want a media product that involves labour, someone, somewhere has to pay for it. With globalisation we have ever-greater quantities of information, we have extended our ability to follow global news in real time from almost anywhere. It is important however, not to mistake abundance for sustainability.

An explosive level of voluntary mobilisation occurred as part of the Yes campaign during the Scottish referendum. It could be seen in blogs, on social media, in town halls, at gigs: indeed in every social space. Nothing like it had ever before been seen in Scotland's history and, indeed, there is not much in Scotland's history that suggests the Scots are particularly disposed to mass mobilisation. If anything, the country has been a deferential society of loyal tribes for much of its existence. All of that changed and a major precursor for that change, the innovative spark that set much of Scotland on the path of creating a mass, spontaneous social movement in 2014, was social media. This is why, before and after the referendum, vast swathes of the British and Scottish establishment were totally unable to comprehend what was going on. Due to its refusal to understand the new spaces of autonomy and the power of the network, those advocating the status quo were caught off balance. Large numbers of people were able to communicate, organise and mobilise without validation, cash or guidance from above. But these platforms are now fragile, they are run by small numbers of people, mostly for little or no remuneration. Stewart Kirkpatrick, Head of Digital at Yes Scotland, raises a cautionary point about the crowdfunding model: 'The things that people will crowdfund are things that they tend to feel passionate about, they tend to feel passionate about things on the same side as they are, it's quite difficult to get people to be passionate about funding something that will disagree at times with their political view.' The path to turning a movement into a wider, normalised, culture of autonomous people searching for original journalism and ideas is not a simple one. For starters, there needs to be a move towards subscribers rather than donors. It's also noticeable that many crowdfunders position themselves as serving a wider cause, that of building an alternative media, rather than simply providing a product or service. It's a point that's picked up by Iain Macwhirter,

> I am depressed by the proliferation of crowdfunding and other forms of charitable fundraising models. Journalism shouldn't be a charity. I hope that a way can be found to put the various Scottish social media ventures on a secure footing, with a degree of independence. There is a danger that you try to appeal to the prejudices of the people who will donate to your venture.

The vast sums of money involved in creating a thorough, regular, multi channel news service are, realistically, far beyond what even the most successful crowdfunded projects in Scotland have achieved. The model is most effective as a vehicle for the creation of a discrete product that a donor has an interest in eventually consuming (as can be seen in the origins of crowdfunding in the independent film industry). The dynamic of providing a comprehensive service, even in an online capacity, is completely different. The real challenge is to find out if a fully fledged alternative news service can be sustained in Scotland. As Ian Bell bluntly reminds us, 'there's no such thing as free in journalism. Free is just another word for hobby. New outlets seeking a wider audience should remember this: the one thing the public can't abide is amateurism. Anyone can tell a story badly.'

Conclusion

> ...it was seldom appreciated that whatever the 'age' similar issues were raised concerning the relationship of 'ownership' of the media to 'content' of 'content' to 'structure' and of 'structure' to technology. All were bound up with 'control'. The need for information in every age has been associated with the effort to control the present and future for personal, political and economic reasons. [256]

Asa Briggs and Peter Burke, *A Social History of the Media* [257]

You don't have to be trying to win a referendum against one the world's most powerful states to realise that information and the control of it are inherently political concerns. The development of new media at any point in history and the opportunities this presents for new techniques to both liberate and control, means that advances in communication technologies have tended to leave massive, systemic change in their wake. The basic mistake is to assume that because the internet allows distribution to occur at virtually no cost, media has somehow become free too. This is not the case. The time, the effort, the creativity and the skill set are unchanged. In Scotland we have discovered the power of the network, and on such a foundation it is possible to build a great deal. It may offer a platform, perhaps even the beginnings of much needed infrastructure, but it is not, in and of itself, a solution. We might want to totally alter some of the practices and cultures that have traditionally defined journalism, we may also want to ensure that a broader cross-section of society is involved in the news making process. However, the real challenge that the information age has brought with it is a greater need for journalists – those who sift through vast swathes of information and re-present it to a wider audience. To do so with skill and professionalism is absolutely inherent to the nature of the task. This was a point picked up by Arnold Kemp in his 1996 lecture on the future of the Scottish press, in which he foresaw the impasse that now faces us:

> Information seems as infinite as the universe. But infinity is incomprehensible and information is of no use to anyone unless it is organised and synthesised. A newspaper does precisely that: a newspaper is the selection and organisation of information into a user-friendly format. And since no newspaper can be all things to all men, the press is, and should be, varied: it should reflect the mosaic of human needs, interests, aspirations and abilities.[258]

What Ithiel de Sola Pool first described in 1983 as 'convergence': the process of communications technologies becoming intertwined and then controlled by a small number of large media organisations with limited competition or accountability, is now more topical than ever. The internet offers a constant negotiation between freedom and control and de Sola Pool's remarks on media structure flag this prescient question, 'Freedom is fostered when the means of communication are dispersed, decentralized, and easily available, as are printing presses and microcomputers. Central control is more likely when the means of communication are concentrated, monopolised, and scarce, as are great networks.'[259] A conflict over control of the public sphere has therefore become a constant feature of our times. Joshua Meyrowitz on the other hand, is optimistic and likens our age to that of our far distant ancestors, untroubled by the interference of controlling structures:

> Many of the features of our 'Information Age' make us resemble the most primitive of social and political forms:

the hunting and gathering society. As nomadic peoples, hunters and gatherers have no loyal relationship to territory. They, too, have little "sense of place"; specific activities are not totally fixed to specific physical settings. The lack of boundaries both in hunting and gathering and in electronic societies leads to many striking parallels. Of all known social types before our own, hunting and gathering societies have tended to be the most egalitarian in terms of the roles of males and females, children and others, and leaders and followers.[260]

While much has been written about the liberating properties of digital media, the reality is far more mixed, as the Media Reform Coalition has pointed out: 'Online news consumption has been converging around traditional news brands for some time.' Rather than looking to alternative providers, overwhelmingly news is sought online from outlets like the BBC, Sky News, and the *Daily Mail*. This brings us back to the difficult question about the decline of the press itself, as Robin MacPherson pointed out: in a Scotland that has always imported vast swathes of its media from elsewhere, the traditional newspaper and publishing industries are a rare example of an autonomous Scottish public sphere,

Print media is the one area which, broadly speaking, has been much more clearly differentiated for much longer, therefore arguably at least has a fighting chance of remaining to be so. My question is, will that remain the case in a digital age, and with a generation for whom, the local, national, global boundaries are becoming porous. So will we end up getting all the news we need about Scotland from the *Huffington Post*?'

The most radical aspect of the case for a Scottish media is not to simply to opt out of anything that purports to be of mainstream origin. Rather, it is to understand that the answer has to be found in restructuring the media in an image more reflective of the changed Scotland that we now inhabit. This does not mean less journalism. Far from it, it means a broad societal commitment to the work of selecting and understanding an abundance of information in an age when it seems to constantly threaten to overpower us. The response to convergence, of media being made by a smaller number of corporations and an elite cadre of professionals, is not to forget the basic societal good of journalism. Instead it is to seek to unlock it from the control of a small number of distant, poorly managed and obscure organisations. As our lives become increasingly *mediated* and the importance of information and access to it increases, we need a new concept of rights to media access, media plurality, and media transparency.

The more awkward question that follows on from the blossoming of new media, is whether the massive collective good-will that sustained pro-independence efforts can be maintained. While it seems possible that new platforms offer alternatives to media practices inherently biased towards the powerful, on the whole, they've yet to offer comprehensive media services that can rival old media bastions. Therefore, if we do want dissenting voices to be heard, we must accept that such questions point towards a need for vast, *structural*, change. The scale of this task is monumental: to restore vitality to the media in Scotland and to upgrade it, to create something new that is broader and more inclusive. This has to be carried out on a non-partisan basis. All of Scottish society needs a renewed media culture in which genuine dialogue and innovation can take place. For in reality, this is not just an issue for those who want Scotland to be a nation state: the question is far more acute than that. It's an issue that must be addressed by all who want to secure Scotland's long term ability to function as a modern democracy.

We need to start thinking of media diversity as a citizenship right, as a basic tenet for democratic participation and be candid about how the market has failed in this regard. In Scotland we have the network to build, not an alternative, but a better, more vibrant media for all. Such a media would be defined by quality *and* diversity. As a nation we now need to be brave enough to create and fund the content to make this a reality. We have the network, the beginnings of a means of distribution: but it is not yet clear whether Scotland's alternative media has the ability to take possession of the means of media production.

Conclusion

Towards a Scottish Media

Communication integrates knowledge, organization and power and runs as a thread linking the earliest memory of man to his noblest aspirations through constant striving for a better life. As the world has advanced, the task of communication has become ever more complex and subtle – to contribute to the liberation of mankind from want, oppression and fear and to unite it in community and communion, solidarity and understanding. However, unless some basic structural changes are introduced, the potential benefits of technological and communication development will hardly be put at the disposal of the majority of mankind.

UNESCO, *Many Voices One World*, 1980 [261]

If this volume has had one single aim it is to be the basis for a far wider set of conversations. This book is a call, above all else, for better dialogue, both in the general sense of a more varied, richer, public sphere and in terms of the specific debate we need to start having about our media. These matters are simply too important to remain the domain of an obscure, distant, professional elite. The shape of the better Scottish media that many of us know to be possible cannot be defined in the committee rooms of New Broadcasting House and Westminster, or, for that matter, those at Holyrood or Pacific Quay.

There is, I think, one crucial point that can become easily lost when looking at the structural anomalies identified above. People will almost invariably use the best media that is available to them, that which is most effective at representing their lives, their politics, their identity and self-image. Therefore the kind of media that this book has argued for is not one that simply ticks a set of boxes to match a quota. This is about much more than good governance, it's about a foundational commitment to quality and plurality. We cannot simply campaign for a Scottish media as we did for a parliament even if the salience of the matter is just as great. Instead, we must argue for the creation of a mediascape that would engage a whole society. There is no point putting in place the immense structural changes, or mustering the vast reserves of political will required to rebuild a truly Scottish public sphere, if, as has been the case all too often, we simply create Scottish content as a chore or ritual. If we cannot move beyond this provincial mindset that underpins how our media operates, we will have wasted our time. The first task in moving towards a new Scottish media is therefore a psychological shift in priorities and perspectives.

This is not simply about the great challenge of viewing Scotland as a democratic space that must be reshaped over the coming years. A new Scottish media must also be built on the premise that the quality with which it is realised, like a nation itself, has to be re-built, re-imagined, re-presented, on a day to day basis. In asserting the right to a Scottish media, we will be pushing against decades of concentration and centralisation of media power. This makes the challenge all the more significant. The concentration of media ownership is a crucial part of a wider process in the global economy, which has seen profits privatised and globalised, while losses have been socialised and localised. Our fear of parochialism: a unit of control which might not be completely abstracted from the domain of collective agency, is the servant of this impoverished world view. We must therefore come to understand that media products are always far more than just private assets, or bureau-cratic outcomes. We must also remember that it is always in the interests of large media organisations to limit the scope of debate and to promote the idea that places like Scotland are homogenous and singular. Such a view sees an entire country defined by a single audience, a single demographic, an easily catered to group of consumer tastes, the subject of simple, manageable stories.

The UNESCO document quoted above (commonly referred to as the MacBride report) reminds us that the basic utility of commu-nication is crucial to our common humanity. It cannot and should not be the property of a single state, corporation or special interest group within society. Instead its diversity must be founded on the right of all not just to access media, but to demand a media ecology that has room for their own identities and cultures within it. Inci-dentally, the report was slammed by the UK government, who would later withdraw from UNESCO in protest at its radical call for the democratic shaping of communicative power and space.[262] An objection to any form of non-market control has defined the broad framework of communications policy and set the terms of the debate for far too long. Long enough, at least, for us to realise that a free market does not mean a free press. A new wave of vast technological change demands new terms, new ideas and a deeper search for solutions.

The central flaw in the market led approach is its basic assump-tion that there is only a binary choice (state or private sector) when it comes to media control, but also glosses over the significant and well documented cultures of silencing, censoring and outright persecu-tion so clearly exposed within commercially funded media. In the UK fear of government interference in a heavily centralised state has tended to blot out the fact that, in a European context at least, the UK is an exception in refusing to maintain basic constitutional or democratic oversight over its press in terms of ownership. This question, for Scotland, needs to be paired up with that of funding as the indigenous press continues in its increasingly frantic dance for survival. Press subsidy is a reality in several European countries and there is no reason, beyond a lack of political will, that it could not work in Scotland. In terms of the objections to such a move: once we get past the inevitable filibustering about statist control and authoritarianism that any discussion of media plurality must sit through, we are left with a deep ideological blindness. Like all empires in decline, those of corporate media control conceive of all alternatives as absurd because they are too preoccupied with their own desperate struggle to maintain legitimacy.

As we have seen, the alienation created by coverage of the referendum was a part of this process, symptomatic of the kind of chaos and loss of purpose that crises can so easily bring about. Confronted with such a democratic surge, facilitated in part by new media with its innate capacity for group formation and low level organising, the media in Scotland were frightened. For the most part, they retreated from this wave of change and reverted to their comfort zones and tired tropes that could muddy, but not stem the tide of a popular movement. This is not, however, simply about the innate conservatism of Scotland's media in crisis mode, it is about longer-term structural issues. Scotland's media began to suffer serious neglect just when we needed it most. The only logical response to that must in turn be structural, but it must not be built from above. The impetus and the tools must come from the ground up. Looked at from such a perspective it becomes easier to conceive of Scotland as a site of opportunity rather than dereliction.

Already, the realm in which freedom is being most tested is immaterial. Key forms of production are no longer simply physical but are becoming increasingly dominated by informational products and ideas. As Scotland seeks to position itself in a shifting landscape of new freedoms and new constraints brought about by the information society, we should also consider the importance of software, the promotion of open source platforms, media commons and the emerging concept of a 'Digital Public Space' as pioneered by BBC iPlayer founder Tony Ageh. This concept marries equality of access to broadband with traditional public service broadcasting values: unmetered consumption of digital content held and protected in the public interest.[263]

The technological question is still in a sense the most prominent. It is not yet clear, on balance, whether the spaces offered by online media will actually be able to provide a sustainable model for increased plurality and alternative narratives. The problem here is also about what underpins Scotland's new media, other than a few small examples of crowdfunded success, the longer-term viability of media production online is not guaranteed and carries with it a new set of challenges. A broader commitment to these networks is required and this should move hand in hand with the need to re-think the broadcast and print media landscape. Both the old and new media ought to be able to learn and interact with each other on mutually beneficial terms. Strange though this might seem today – it is surely inevitable in the longer term.

All of this considered, there remains once inescapable point: to accept Scotland's media in its current state is to risk not just future opportunities to move forward but also to undo or embitter many of the changes that have already taken place. To accept Scotland's democratic media deficit is to accept Scotland's public life as a half-life, defined primarily by an archaic silence and clichéd novelty.

As I said at the start of this book, there is no simple solution to such a complex problem. But if there is something to aim for, it must be to make a national media that isn't just fit for purpose, but that is as good as it possibly can be. Such a media would be defined by the diversity and freedom of online media *and* the quality of the best of our traditions.

In the twenty-first century we are poised, in this place and all others, to face up to irrevocable changes: to take multiple steps into the haar that we are unlikely to be able to retrace. We cannot ask for a map as the destination is uncertain. We cannot ask for more time. Any form of insurance policy is out of the question. But the one thing that we can ask, the one clear demand, must be to take these steps with as much self-awareness, as much collective memory, as much knowledge and as much insight as we can carry with us. If this all sounds a bit too fanciful – just consider the prospect of standing still.

25 Ideas to Reboot Scotland's Media

The title of this book stems from the idea that Scotland could achieve something unique by building a popular, quality media as the result of a broad based democratic process. The answers will not be found in any single volume, but rather in the kind of processes that any mature democracy should value: public debate, crowdsourcing and citizen led participation. The following ideas for action are offered in that spirit. All such changes are contingent on a radical reorganisation of political priorities in Scotland to place media and culture at the forefront of Scotland's continuing democratic adventure. History shows that a nation without a state can continue to exist, even flourish, if the conditions are correct. A nation without a media on the other hand – that struggles to communicate with itself or with the wider world – faces a far more complex predicament. Perhaps one of the most productive ways in which the engagement channelled into the Scottish referendum might be called upon once again, is through a proactive, positive and inclusive movement for the right to a Scottish media. Like our search for a parliament, the route will be long and frequently compromised, but once established as a new reality no one will want to go back to the suffocating neglect of being represented elsewhere.

1. A Charter of Media Rights is drawn up which will serve, in the absence of a written constitution, to state levels of provision and access across all media channels. This would be based on a public consultation with citizens and media professionals. It will establish a commitment to plurality and to nurturing Scottish talent.

2. The Charter Renewal process sees the BBC adopt a federal structure: devolving key commissioning powers to Scotland and expanding BBC Scotland's budget significantly. This would meet already mooted plans for a dedicated Scottish TV channel and an improved radio service.

3. BBC Scotland adopts an open, decentralised and creatively led commissioning process for original programming in Scotland that would be founded on a specific commitment to reflect life all across the country, not just Glasgow and the central belt.

4. A New Media Trust is set up involving several different elements. Independent of government, it will promote the distribution of accessible media and journalism that fulfils a public service role in Scotland. This will offer competition for traditional news media, but also much needed infrastructure, resources, training and development opportunities. It will foster professional links between old and new media outlets. Such a body could act as a bridge to ensure that expertise is channelled into new media operations (through mentoring schemes, for example) while also allowing newspapers and broadcast media to benefit from the ideas and diversity present in online media.

5. An independent film agency for Scotland is set up with a budget that allows it to compete with the Irish Film Board and Northern

Ireland Screen.

6. A Scottish film studio is founded that offers discounted access to local productions and with specifically allotted space for TV drama production. The combination of an agency and studio allows Scotland to move towards a target based on a regular number of feature films to be produced each year.

7. Control of broadcasting is devolved to the Scottish Parliament, which should then immediately devolve control to an external body that can bring together different sectorial interests, media and the BBC's Audience Council Scotland.

8. A scheme based on the Canadian Content system is created, within a new Scottish Broadcasting Act. It specifies a set amount of prime time programming must originate in Scotland. This could, for example, consist of at least one original weekly Scottish drama or extended current affairs coverage. Such a measure would have an in-built commitment to quality and variety.

9. A set number of graduate places across the Scottish media are guaranteed for the hundreds of journalism and film graduates leaving Scottish universities each year.

10. A New Deal for Digital commits to ending the digital divide in Scotland by rolling out superfast broadband. This would encourage connectivity in rural areas and areas of multiple deprivation.

11. This is accompanied by a programme of community media education and the promotion of socially productive online media.

12. Scotland emulates the culture tax policies of the French government: to set up a fund to reimburse local and national news

services for their online content and to support national film and TV production. This should include levies on online streaming providers like Netflix, Amazon and Google.

13. Local media is revived: the Scottish Government, local authorities and NGOs join together to establish a basic minimum level of local media provision throughout Scotland. This not only provides increased opportunities for journalists but also breaks up the monopolies in local media ownership.

14. This could be modelled on local media provision in areas like Orkney and Shetland: a nightly public service opt-out local news programme on Radio Scotland and at least two independent outlets for local journalism. In many areas this would allow community media ventures to expand and professionalise their operations.

15. Modelled on Norway's Mass Media Authority, Scotland sets up a scheme for press subsidy for news operations of all sizes.

16. This is contingent on adherence to a new Editor's Code, which embodies values such as the gathering of news through direct reporting and the clear separation of comment from opinion.

17. Scotland commits its public and media institutions to supporting the use of open source software, creative commons and supports the creation of a Digital Public Space, founded on equality of access to an archive of publicly held digital material.

18. All cultural and media organisations and businesses operating in Scotland are made exempt from VAT.

19. BBC Radio Scotland is split into at least two dedicated Scottish stations, with one station offering news, current affairs and speech

based content and the other(s) focused on sport and music.

20. A levy is introduced with a similar aim to the French government's long running policy of funding national film production via cinema tickets. This could also encompass tickets for large scale, highly profitable events such as big name concerts, festivals and luxury tourism.

21. Scotland becomes a full national member of UNESCO.

22. Drawing on expertise built up in the video games industry, Scotland becomes a leading centre for media innovation in areas such as second screen technology, interactive and on demand services.

23. The further roll out of local TV services come to act as hubs for a new regional tier of broadcast media in Scotland roughly equivalent to the Scottish Parliament's electoral regions.

24. An independent Scottish news agency, with an international network, is set up as a partnership by several key media organisations in Scotland.

25. Media ownership is limited by setting up a 'public interest test' as outlined by the Media Reform Coalition to restrict the concentration of media ownership. Such a test could include a mandatory minimum level of staffing and resources for each title based in Scotland.

Notes

Introduction

1. Jamies Ross, 'The SNP's Rally Of 12,000 Nationalists Was The Most Bizarre Political Event Of The Year', 22 November 2014 http://www.buzzfeed.com/jamieross/the-snps-rally-with-12000-nationalists-was-the-most-bizarre#.yrrbrljXD Accessed 05 April 2015

2. BBC News, 'Scottish Standard newspaper folds', 25 April 2005, http://news.bbc.co.uk/1/hi/scotland/4483449.stmAccessed 05 April 2015

3. Will Hutton, 'We have 10 days to find a settlement to save the union' 6 September 2014, *Guardian*, 6 September 2014

4. Nicola Sturgeon, 'First Minister Sturgeon on the media and the future of the BBC' 27 August 2015, *NewsNet Scotland*, http://newsnet.scot/?p=115531 Accessed 27 August 2015

1. A Democratic Deficit

5. Manuel Castells, *Communication Power*, (Oxford: OUP, 2013) p. 70

6. Tom Devine, 'Failing the nation? The decline and fall of Radio Scotland' *Scottish Review*, http://www.scottishreview.net/ThomasDevine45.shtml 8 January 2013 Accessed 20 March 2015

7. Gerry Hassan, *Independence of the Scottish Mind: Elite Narratives, Public Spaces and the Making of a Modern Nation*, (London, Palgrave Macmillan, 2014) p. 189

8. Brian McNair, 'The Scottish Media and Politics' *The Media in Scotland*, ed. by Neil Blain and David Hutchison, (Edinburgh, EUP, 2008) p. 239

9. IPSO, 'Editors' Code of Practice' https://www.ipso.co.uk/IPSO/cop.html, Accessed 04 May 2015

10. Hacked Off, 'IPSO – MYTHS AND REALITIES' http://hackinginquiry.
org/the-campaign/the-truth-about-ispo/ipso-myths-and-realities/
Accessed 03 May 2015
Media Standards Trust, ISPO, an assessment by the Media Standards
Trust, 15 November 2013, http://mediastandardstrust.org/mst-news/
ipso-an-assessment-by-the-media-standards-trust/ Accessed 05 May 2015

11. Farhad Manjoo 'You won't finish this article' *Slate,* 06 June 2013 http://
www.slate.com/articles/technology/technology/2013/06/how_
people_read_online_why_you_won_t_finish_this_article.html Accessed
30 May 2015

12. Severin Carrell, 'Whisky maker Diageo fears impact of Scottish independence' *Guardian* 30 May 2014

13. Dominic Walsh, 'Diageo boss wary of Scottish independence impact on
whisky industry', *The Times,* 30 May 2014

14. Magnus Gardham, 'Do it yourself? B&Q chief urges Scots to stick with
the Union' *Herald,* 31 May 2014

15. Ben Riley-Smith, 'How the Union was almost lost: The inside story of
the Scottish independence campaign's last 100 days', *Daily Telegraph,* 27
December 2014

16. Edward S. Herman and Noam Chomsky, *Manufacturing Consent: The
Political Economy of the Mass Media,* Edward S Herman and Noam
Chomsky (London: Vintage, 1994) p. 2

17. Ibid. p. 2

18. Peter Oborne, 'Why I have resigned from the Telegraph' *OurKingdom,* 17
February 2015 https://www.opendemocracy.net/ourkingdom/peter-
oborne/why-i-have-resigned-from-telegraph Accessed 30 March 2015

19. Ian Stewart, 'Friends of The Scotsman: invitation from the Editor',
Scotsman, 5 June 2013

20. Rushabh Haria, 'Newsquest reporter quits after failing to meet six-story
quota while at hospital with terminally ill grandmother', *Press Gazette,*
17 July 2015

21. Media Reform Coalition, *A Case for Action,* http://www.mediareform.
org.uk/wp-content/uploads/2014/11/FULL-PDF.pdf December 2014

22. IPSOS Mori, https://www.ipsos-mori.com/Assets/Docs/Polls/
Veracity%20Index%202014%20topline.pdf Accessed 30 March 2015

23. The Sutton Trust, *Research Brief, Internship or Indenture?*, 2 November 2014, http://www.suttontrust.com/wp-content/uploads/2014/11/Unpaid-Internships.pdf

24. Owen Jones, *The Establishment and How They Got Away With It*, (London: Allen Lane, 2014) p. 100

25. Ibid. p.123

26. Justin Lewis, Andrew Williams, Bob Franklin, James Thomas and Nick Mosdell *The Quality and Independence of British Journalism Tracking the changes over 20 years* (Cardiff: University of Cardiff/Media Wise, 2008) p. 25

27. Nick Davies, *Flat Earth News*, (London: Vintage, 2009) p. 73

28. Andrew Marr, *My Trade*, (Oxford: Macmillan, 2004) p. 384

29. Ben Goldacre, 'Dodgy Academic PR', *Guardian*, 30 May 2009

30. Carolyn M Byerly, *Global Report on the Status of Women in the News Media*, (Washington: International Women's Media Foundation, 2011)

31. Scottish Referendum Study, 'Why Scotland Vote No' http://www.scottishreferendumstudy.com/files/2015/01/RHUL-slides.pdf 30 September 2014 p. 20

32. BBC News, 'Charity urges action over 'growing digital divide'' http://www.bbc.co.uk/news/uk-scotland-scotland-business-25214376 4 December 2013 Accessed 30 March 2015

33. Ben Wray, 'Workers pass vote of no confidence: "We won't be "click-bait" journalists"' *Common Space*, 12 June 2015

34. James Curran and Jean Seaton, *Power Without Responsibility: The Press and Broadcasting in Britain*, (London: Routeledge, 1997) p. 49

35. Jon Snow, 'Nothing Beats the Reporter on the Spot,' *Guardian*, 21 November 2005

36. Digital Spy, 'Watch Jon Snow thank Margaret Thatcher in BAFTA Fellowship speech', http://www.digitalspy.co.uk/tv/news/a646630/watch-jon-snow-thank-margaret-thatcher-in-bafta-fellowship-speech.html#~pjV5WWUaZpkfN5 11 May 2015 Accessed 30 May 2015

37. Lee Bunce, 'Putting Journalism at the Heart of Democracy' *Scotland 44: Ideas for a New Nation* (Edinburgh, Post Collective, 2014)

38. Peter Geoghegan, 'New media model needed to keep Press alive,' *Scotsman*, Thursday 28 March 2013

2. Ten Days to Save Britain

39. Severin Carrell, 'Electoral Commission voids CBI listing as no campaigner in Scotland vote' *Guardian*, 1 May 2014

40. Szu Ping Chan, 'Scottish independence: CBI chairman warns of "enormous" risks with a Yes vote' *Daily Telegraph*, 28 August 2014

41. John Mullin, 'Licence to feel very proud of BBC' *Scotsman*, 17 July 2015

42. STV, 'Audience of 1.7 million tune in to STV Salmond and Darling debate' 6 August 2014

43. Graeme Baxter, 'Analysis of Twitter responses indicates a preference for diversity in televised political debates' *Democratic Audit UK*, 3 July 2015

44. Lesley Riddoch, 'BBC caught in political crossfire', *Scotsman*, 22 June 2014

45. David Patrick, 'Bought and Sold, or Hype in Bold? Newspaper Framing of the Scottish Independence Debate' *BS News* 18 September 2014

46. John Stevens, 'Childless SNP chiefs 'who have no feel for UK family': Leaders of Scottish National Party "want to break up Union because they do not understand families," it is claimed' *Daily Mail*, 13 September 2014

47. John Robertson, 'BBC bias and the Scots referendum - new report' *OurKingdom* 21 February 2014 https://www.opendemocracy.net/ourkingdom/john-robertson/bbc-bias-and-scots-referendum-new-report Accessed 01 April 2015

48. David Miller, 'Taking Sides' *Guardian* 22 April 2003

49. David Edwards & David Cromwell, 'BBC's Iraq coverage - biased or balanced?' *Talk About Newsnight*, 19 March 2007

50. Tony Benn, 'Protest is vital to a thriving democracy' *Independent*, 22 January 2011

51. Stuart Campbell, 'Identity Parade' *Wings Over Scotland*, http://wingsoverscotland.com/identity-parade/ 29 October 2013 Accessed 30 April 2015

52. John Plunkett 'BBC defends coverage of Israeli air strikes in Gaza after bias accusations' *Guardian*, 16 July 2014

53. Tariq Ali, 'After the Referendum' *London Review of Books*, Vol. 36 No. 19, 9 October 2014

54. Chris Green, 'Scottish independence: BBC Scotland's referendum coverage 'institutionally biased', Alex Salmond claims' *Independent*, 14 September 2014

55. Severin Carrell, Nicholas Watt and Patrick Wintour. 'The real story of the Scottish referendum: Britain on the brink' *Guardian*, 15 December 2014

56. 'Blurred Lines' https://www.youtube.com/watch?v=ckLDmwwb5sc 2 May 2014 Accessed 1 May 2015

57. Kieran Andrews, 'Great Ormond Street hospital orders Vote No Borders to bin anti-independence advert' *Courier*, 30 May 2014

58. Pierre Bourdieu, *On Television*, (New York: New Press, 1998) p. 3-4

59. Ibid. p. 10-11

60. Mehdi Hassan, 'Please don't listen to Anjem Choudary' *Guardian*, 4 January 2010

61. Libby Watson, 'Hannity Provides Platform For Anti-Muslim Pam Geller And Extremist Anjem Choudary To Debate' *Media Matters for America*, 6 May 2015

62. http://twitpic.com/5u6n2l Accessed 3 May 2015

63. Chris Abbott, 'As the dust settles: Avoiding the mistakes of Oslo and Utøya in future media coverage of suspected terrorist attacks' *Open Briefing*, http://www.openbriefing.org/thinktank/publications/asthe-dustsettles/ 5 August 2011

64. Asa Briggs and Peter Burke, *Social History of the Media: From Gutenberg to the Internet*, (Cambridge: Polity, 2005) p. 249

65. 'CNN Gulf War Promos 1991' https://www.youtube.com/watch?v=WQhsK0ZUoO4 Accessed 3 May 2015

66. Tilda Swinton, 'A letter from a boy to his mother' *Vertigo*, Vol. 3 Issue 3, Autumn 2006

67. Bourdieu pp. 21-22

68. Neil Postman, *Amusing Ourselves to Death: Public Discourse in the Age of Show Business*, (London: Penguin, 2006), p. 99

69. John Galtung and Mari Ruge, 'Structuring and selecting news' *The Manufacture of News: a Reader*, eds. Stanley Cohen and Jock Young, (London: Constable, 1973)

70. Brian McNair, 'The Scottish Media and Politics' *The Media in Scotland*, ed. by Neil Blain and David Hutchison, (Edinburgh, EUP, 2008) p. 234

71. Scottish Broadcasting Commission, *Platform for Success*, (Edinburgh, Scottish Government, 2008) p. 14

72. Paul Hodkinson, *Media, Culture and Society An Introduction*, (London: Sage, 2011) p. 130

73. AA Gill, 'Argh, it's Game of Skull and Crossbones' *Sunday Times*, 26 July 2015

74. Tom Gordon, 'Indyref minus 200: meeting the Blairs across the Yes/No divide,' *Sunday Herald*, 2 March, 2014

75. George Gerber, 'Reclaiming Our Cultural Mythology: Television's global marketing strategy creates a damaging and alienated window on the world' *In Context*, 38, Spring 1994

76. Lord Ashcroft, 'Post-Referendum Scotland Poll 18-19 September' http://lordashcroftpolls.com/wp-content/uploads/2014/09/Lord-Ashcroft-Polls-Referendum-day-poll-summary-1409191.pdf Accessed 30 May 2015

77. Severin Carrell, Nicholas Watt and Patrick Wintour 'The real story of the Scottish referendum: the final days of the fight for independence' *Guardian*, 16 December 2014

78. YouGov, 'Scotland Trackers Scottish Referendum', http://d25d2506sfb94s.cloudfront.net/cumulus_uploads/document/5lijo88bs3/YG-trackers-Scottish-Referendum-150501.pdf Accessed 30 May 2015

79. Severin Carrell, Nicholas Watt and Patrick Wintour 'The real story of the Scottish referendum: the final days of the fight for independence' *Guardian*, 16 December 2014

80. Elizabeth Rigby, Martin Arnold and Jim Pickard, 'Downing St reception used to goad business chiefs into action', *Financial Times*, 11 September 2014

81. 'Salmond: it's the BBC's unconscious bias which is extraordinary' *Herald*, 14 September 2014

82. 'BBC, Banks, Treasury leak, Alex Salmond, International Media at EICC' https://www.youtube.com/watch?v=cWNkuIBhw3I Accessed 24 March 2014

83. 'Warning of polling station clashes as tensions rise' *Herald*, 01 September 2014

84. Libby Brooks, 'Scotland referendum sides told to keep campaigns civil and peaceful' *Guardian*, 01 September 2014

85. Chris Green, 'Scottish independence referendum: A nation divided against itself' *Independent* 16 September

86. Iain Macwhirter, *Disunited Kingdom: How Westminster Won A Referendum But Lost Scotland* (Glasgow: Cargo, 2014) p. 84

87. Ibid. p. 84

88. Magnus Gardham, 'Support for Yes vote drops to just 25%' *Herald*, 4 September 2014

89. Maggie Brown and Jason Dean, 'Robert Peston: BBC follows the Daily Mail's lead too much' *Guardian* Friday 6 June 2014

90. David Patrick, 'Bought and Sold, or Hype in Bold? Newspaper Framing of the Scottish Independence Debate' *BS News* 18 September 2014

91. Stephen Daisley, '28 quotes from the Alan Cochrane diaries we genuinely did not make up' *STV* 14 December 2014

92. Stuart Campbell 'Taking the Biscuit' *Wings Over Scotland*, 04 October 2014, http://wingsoverscotland.com/taking-the-biscuits/ Accessed 01 April 2015

93. Michael Billig, *Banal Nationalism* (London: Sage, 1995). p. 11

94. Sunday Herald View, 'the prize for Yes is a better country...it is as simple as that' *Sunday Herald*, 4 May 2014

3. British Broadcasting

95. Ernest Gellner, *Nations and Nationalism: New Perspectives on the Past,* (Oxford: Blackwell, 1994) p. 127

96. Asa Briggs and Peter Burke, *Social History of the Media: From Gutenberg to the Internet,* (Cambridge: Polity, 2005) p. 130

97. 'The unlikely revolutionary', *Economist*, 12 August 2010

98. Paul Hodkinson, *Media, Culture and Society: An Introduction,* (London: Sage, 2011) p. 178

99. Asa Briggs and Peter Burke, *Social History of the Media: From Gutenberg to the Internet*, (Cambridge: Polity, 2005) p. 188

100. David Cannadine, 'The Context, Performance and Meaning of Ritual: The British Monarchy and the 'Invention of Tradition', c.1820-1977' in *The Invention of Tradition*, ed. by Eric Hobsbawn and Trever Roper, (Cambridge: Canto, 1992) pp. 101-164 p. 159

101. OFCOM, 'Ofcom review of public service television broadcasting,' 15 June 2004 http://stakeholders.ofcom.org.uk/binaries/consultations/psb/annexes/157377.pdf p.10

102. Nigel Morris, 'David Cameron aims to harness the 'Team GB' spirit to beat back support for Scottish independence' *Independent* 7 February 2014

103. Department for Media Culture and Sport, *Review of the BBC's Royal Charter, A strong BBC, independent of government*, 2 March 2005 http://news.bbc.co.uk/1/shared/bsp/hi/pdfs/02_03_05_bbcgreen.pdf p.2

104. Charlotte Higgins, 'The battle for the BBC', *Guardian*, 14 July 2015

105. BBC News, 'BBC Green Paper: Key points' 16 July 2015 http://www.bbc.co.uk/news/entertainment-arts-33556009 Accessed 30 July 2015

106. BBC Trust, *BBC Annual Report and Accounts*, 14 July 2015 http://downloads.bbc.co.uk/annualreport/pdf/2014-15/bbc-annualreport-201415.pdf

107. Maggie Sweeney, 'Broadcasting from Birth to Devolution and Beyond' *The Media in Scotland*, ed. by Neil Blain and David Hutchison, (Edinburgh, EUP, 2008) p. 101

108. Neil Blain and David Hutchison, 'A Cause Still Unwon: The Struggle to Represent Scotland' *The Media in Scotland*, ed. by Neil Blain and David Hutchison, (Edinburgh, EUP, 2008) p. 14

109. Gerry Hassan, 'Nation to Nation: The Problem of Speaking for Britain,' 29 October 2010 http://www.gerryhassan.com/blog/nation-to-nation-the-problem-of-speaking-for-britain/ Accessed 05 May 2015

110. 'Ian Davidson accuses Isabel Fraser and BBC of pro-SNP bias on Newsnight Scotland' 7 August 2012 https://www.youtube.com/watch?v=nnUuwIgqWO4 Accessed 20 March 2015

111. George McKechnie, 'Nationalism and the BBC' *Scottish Review of Books*, Vol. 9 Issue 3 2013

112. Alasdair Milne, *DG, Memoirs of a British Broadcaster,* (London: Hodder & Stoughton 1988) pp. 66-67

113. David Pat Walker, *The BBC in Scotland: the first 50 years,* (Edinburgh, Luath, 2011) p. 256

114. Jean Seaton, *Pinkoes and Traitors, The BBC and the Nation,* 1974-1987, (London: Profile Books, 2015) p. 2

115. Alastair Hetherington, *Inside BBC Scotland, 1975-80: A Personal View,* (Aberdeen: Whitewater, 1992) p. 2

116. Ibid. p. 5

117. Kenneth Roy, 'Beebus Scotticus' *Scottish Review of Books,* Vol. 7 Issue 4, November 2011.

118. Alexander Grant, 'BBC Scotland staff in row over window blinds' *Scotsman* 22 July 2014 22 July 2014

119. *The BBC in Scotland,* p. 257

120. Quoted in Gerry Hassan, *Independence of the Scottish Mind: Elite Narratives, Public Spaces and the Making of a Modern Nation,* (London, Palgrave Macmillan, 2014) p. 79

121. 'Why I would have resigned: John McCormick, BBC Scotland controller, is poised to retire, but his departure could have been abrupt' *Herald,* 19 March 2004

122. *Independence of the Scottish Mind: Elite Narratives, Public Spaces and the Making of a Modern Nation,* pp. 78-80

123. Tom Devine, 'Failing the nation?:The decline and fall of Radio Scotland' *Scottish Review,* 8 January 2013, http://www.scottishreview.net/ThomasDevine45.shtml Accessed 20 March 2015

124. BBC News, 'BBC Radio Scotland announces changes to its schedule' 16 December 2014 http://www.bbc.co.uk/news/uk-scotland-30505342

125. 'Fears BBC will cut more jobs as head of news quits Corporation refuses to rule out axe claims' *Herald,* 13 July 2006

126. Scottish Parliament, *Official Report, Education and Culture Committee,* 24 January 2012 http://www.scottish.parliament.uk/parliamentarybusiness/report.aspx?r=6909&mode=pdf pp.650-651

127. Severin Carrell, 'BBC Scotland news boss moves jobs after strike threats over bullying claims' *Guardian,* 16 June 2015

128. John Birt, *The Harder Path, the Autobiography,* (London: Time Warner, 2003) p. 483

129. Ibid. pp. 483-484

130. 'Why I would have resigned' *Herald,* 19 March 2004

131. 'London vetoes BBC's Scottish news' *Herald,* 21 November 1998

132. Joan McAlpine, 'Why did the media lose its Scottish accent of the mind?' in *Radical Scotland Arguments for Self-Determination,* eds Gerry Hassan and Rosie Ilett, pp. 222-238

133. Phantom Power, Protest Against BBC Scotland Referendum Bias 2 29 June 2014 https://www.youtube.com/watch?v=7Hk1o2Apa_Q Accessed 15 March 2015

134. David Elstein, 'Broadcasting for Scotland' *OurKingdom,* 18 September 2013 https://www.opendemocracy.net/ourkingdom/david-elstein/broadcasting-for-scotland Accessed 01 April 2015

135. Scottish Broadcasting Commission, *Platform for Success,* (Edinburgh, Scottish Government, 2008) p. 20

136. BBC Trust, *BBC Annual Report and Accounts,* 14 July 2015 http://downloads.bbc.co.uk/annualreport/pdf/2014-15/bbc-annualreport-201415.pdf p. 26

4. The Cultural Case

137. Mark Thompson, 'Speech given at opening of BBC Scotland's new headquarters at Pacific Quay, Glasgow' http://www.bbc.co.uk/pressoffice/speeches/stories/thompson_pq.shtml 20 September 2014

138. David McCrone, *Understanding Scotland: The Sociology of a Nation,* (London: Routledge, 2001) p. 214

139. 'Grade Scottish TV Suffering from shortage of talent' *Sunday Herald,* 1 July 2007

140. Scottish Parliament, *Official Report Education and Culture Committee,* http://www.scottish.parliament.uk/parliamentarybusiness/report.aspx?r=7283&mode=pdf 29 May 2012

141. BBC News, 'BBC switches Waterloo Road production to Scotland' 23 August 2011 http://www.bbc.co.uk/news/uk-scotland-glasgow-west-14629725 Accessed 01 May 2015

142. 'Stars shocked as Waterloo Road moves to Scotland' *Manchester Evening News*, 24 August 2011

143. Eleanor Yule & David Manderson *The Glass Half Full Moving Beyond Scottish Miserablism* (Edinburgh: Luath, 2014) pp. 68-69

144. Ibid. p. 17 pp. 69-70

145. Tom Nairn, *The Break-up of Britain*, (London: Verso, 1981) p. 150

146. Ibid. p.155

147. Yule and Manderson, pp. 16-17

148. Teddy Jamieson, 'Drawn to the Dark Side' *Herald*, 13 November 2011

149. Jamie Dunn, 'Cine Caledonia – A New Dawn' *Skinny* 1 October 2013

150. Craig Austin, 'MULTIPLE REGENERATION: DR WHO, WALES AND THE RENAISSANCE OF INGENIOUS TELEVISION' *Wales Arts Review* http://www.walesartsreview.org/longform-multiple-regeneration-dr-who-wales-and-the-renaissance-of-ingenious-television/, 14 October 2012 Accessed 30 May 2015

151. Phil Miller, 'Beaten in Game of Thrones: why Scotland lost £160m chance to host TV series,' *Herald*, 17 June 2013

152. Brian Ferguson, 'Taskforce call for Scotland's ailing film industry' *Scotsman*, 21 January 2015

153. McCrone, p. 145

154. Andrew Eaton Lewis, 'Celtic Connections Cures Cultural Cringe' *Scotland on Sunday*, 12 January 2014

155. BBC News 'Armando Iannucci: Britain needs a strong TV industry' 26 August 2015 http://www.bbc.co.uk/news/entertainment-arts-34064794 Accessed 26 August 2015

156. The James Plays trilogy to tour in 2016, *The Stage,* 23 June 2015

157. 'Changin Scotland March 2015. International Connections: Culture and Soft Power' https://www.mixcloud.com/LochbroomFM/changin-scotland-mar-2015-international-connections-culture-and-soft-power/ Accessed 10 June 2015

158. Cairns Craig, *The Modern Scottish Novel, Narrative and the National Imagination,* (Edinburgh: EUP, 1999). p. 12

159. Cultural Commission, *Final Report*, 23 June 2005 http://www.gov.scot/

Resource/Doc/54357/0013577.pdf p.1

160. Fiona Hyslop 'On Scottish culture' *Scotsman*, 5 July 2013

161. Scottish National Party, *Manifesto 2015*, http://votesnp.com/docs/manifesto.pdf p.21

162. Gerard Gilbert, 'How does Danish TV company DR keep churning out the hits?' *Independent* 12 May 2012

163. Mark Lawson 'Are we really in a 'second golden age for television'?' *Guardian*, 23 May 2013

164. Noe Mendelle, Lessons from Denmark, Scottish Documentary Blog, http://blog.scottishdocinstitute.com/lessons_from_denmark 15 February 2012 Accesed 30 May 2014

165. David Bruce 'The history of film and cinema' *The Media in Scotland*, ed. by Neil Blain and David Hutchison, (Edinburgh, EUP, 2008) p. 81

166. Robin McPherson, 'Scottish film industry is in permanent crisis' *Scotsman*, 12 March 2015

167. Andrew O'Hagan, 'Civic Memory: Making Scotlands of the Mind' *National Theatre of Scotland, Fifth Birthday Lecture*, 24 August 2011

168. Patrick Kavanagh, 'The Parish and the Universe', *Collected Prose*, (London: MacGibbon & Kee, 1967) p. 252

169. 'Scotland: a Cultural Affirmation' http://www.culturalaffirmation.scot Accessed 05 June 2015

170. Quoted in Yule, p. 71

5. Being Thought Independent

171. Andrew Marr, *My Trade*, (Oxford: Macmillan, 2004) pp. xviii-xix

172. Roy Greenslade, 'Johnston Press saves £1m a year with office move for The Scotsman' *Guardian* 28 April 2014

173. Maurice Smith, *Paper lions: the Scottish press and national identity*, (Edinburgh: Polygon, 1994) p. 2

174. Brian McNair, 'News from a small country' in *Local Journalism and Local Media*, ed. Bob Franklin (London Routledge 2006) pp. 37-49

175. Arnold Kemp and Jackie Kemp, *Confusion to Our Enemies: Selected*

Journalism of Arnold Kemp (1939-2002) (Glasgow: Neil Wilson Publishing, 2013) p. 29

176. Jack Goody, *Literature in Traditional Societies*, (Cambridge, Cambridge University Press, 1975) pp. 32-33

177. Marshall McLuhan, *The Gutenberg Galaxy*, (Toronto: University of Toronto Press, 2011) p. 155

178. National Library of Scotland 'First Scottish Books' http://digital.nls.uk/firstscottishbooks/place.html (2006)

179. Quoted in R.A Houston, *Scottish Literacy and the Scottish Identity: Illiteracy and Society in Scotland and Northern England, 1600-1800* (Cambridge, Cambridge University Press, 2002) p. 79

180. Leith Davies, *Back to the Future: Negotiating Scottish Sites of Memory, 1707/2014* (Glasgow: Association for Scottish Literary Studies, 2014) p. 8

181. R M Cowan, *The Newspaper in Scotland, a history of its first expansion 1815-1860* (Glasgow: George Outram, 1946) p. 3

182. Asa Briggs and Peter Burke, *A Social History of the Media: From Gutenberg to the Internet*, (Cambridge: Polity, 2005) p. 60

183. Jürgen Habermas, *The Structural Transformation of the Public Sphere: An Inquiry Into a Category of Bourgeois Society* (New York, John Wiley and Sons, 2015) p. xi

184. David Hutchison, 'The History of the Press', *The Media in Scotland*, ed. by Neil Blain and David Hutchison, (Edinburgh, EUP, 2008) pp. 57-58

185. Benedict Anderson, *Imagined Communities: Reflections on the Origin and Spread of Nationalism*, (London: Verso, 2006) p. 26

186. Tom Devine, *The Scottish Nation: A Modern History*, (London: Penguin, 2012) p. 62

187. '30 June 1855: Newspaper stamp duty abolished', *From the Archive Blog*, http://www.theguardian.com/theguardian/from-the-archive-blog/2011/may/10/guardian190-newspaper-duty-cut

188. David Hutchison, 'The History of the Press', *The Media in Scotland*, ed. by Neil Blain and David Hutchison, (Edinburgh, EUP, 2008) p. 61

189. Brian McNair, 'The Scottish Media and Politics' *The Media in Scotland*, ed. by Neil Blain and David Hutchison, (Edinburgh, EUP, 2008) p. 237

190. William Donaldson, *Popular literature in Victorian Scotland: language, fiction and the press* (Aberdeen: Aberdeen University Press, 1986) p. 148

191. Murray Pittock, *The Road to Independence? Scotland in the Balance* (London: Reaktion Books, 2014) p. 20

192. James Barke, 'The Scottish National Question' in *Modernism and Nationalism, Literature and Society in Scotland 1918-1939,* Ed. Margery Palmer McCulloch, (Glasgow: Association for Scottish Literary Studies, 2004) pp. 367-370

193. Kemp, p. 52

194. Harry Reid, *Deadline: The Story of the Scottish Press,* (Edinburgh: St Andrews Press 2006) p. xv

195. Ibid. pp. 94-95

196. Karl Wolfgang Deutsch, *Nationalism and Social Communication: An Inquiry Into the Foundations of Nationality,* (Cambridge, MA: MIT Press, 1966) p. 97

197. Benedict Anderson, *Imagined Communities: Reflections on the Origin and Spread of Nationalism,* (London: Verso, 2006) pp. 35-36

198. Reid, p. 15

199. Magnus Linklater, 'Emphatically not their finest hour' *British Journalism Review* Vol. 25, No. 2, 2014, pp. 26-29

200. Hassan, *Independence of the Scottish Mind* p. 188

201. Smith, p. 15

202. Iain Macwhirter, *Democracy in the Dark: The Decline of the Scottish Press and How to Keep the Lights On* Saltire Series No. 5, (Edinburgh: Saltire Society, 2014) p. 18

203. STV, 'The Buck Stops Here - Alan Taylor,' https://www.youtube.com/watch?v=VqDJSB7tRAE 14 August 2010

204. Cairns Craig, 'The Case for Culture' *Scottish Review of Books,* Vol 10 No. 3 2014

205. Fiona Douglas, *Scottish Newspapers, Language and Identity* (Edinburgh University Press, 2009) pp. 154-155

206. Joan McAlpine, 'Why did the media lose its Scottish accent of the

mind?' in *Radical Scotland Arguments for Self-Determination*, eds Gerry Hassan and Rosie Ilett, pp. 223

207. Kemp, p. 53

208. Hassan p. 73

209. David Hutchison, 'If Scotland votes no, the media may well get the blame' *The Conversation*, 20 June 2014 http://theconversation.com/if-scotland-votes-no-the-media-may-well-get-the-blame Accessed 07 May 2015

210. Brian Taylor, *Scotland's Parliament, Triumph and Disaster*, (Edinburgh: EUP, 2002) p. 10

211. George Rosie, 'Coming adrift on the Mound' *New Statesman*, 20 March 2000

212. Alex Massie, 'The Scottish press is fighting for its life' *Think Scotland* 19 March 2013 http://www.thinkscotland.org/todays-thinking/articles.html?read_full=12024 Accessed 30 April 2015

213. Douglas, p. 51

214. Arthur MacMillan 'The sad decline of The Scotsman' *British Journalism Review* Vol. 23, No. 4, 2012, pp. 64-69

215. Philip Meyer, *The Vanishing Newspaper [2nd Ed]: Saving Journalism in the Information Age* (Columbia: University of Missouri Press, 2009) p. 43

216. John McGurk, 'TIME TO PUT THE SCOTSMAN OUT OF ITS MISERY' *ScottBuzz* http://scot-buzz.co.uk/time-put-scotsman-misery/ Accessed 24 April 2015

217. MacMillan, p. 64

218. *The Press and Journal Media Pack*, https://www.pressandjournal.co.uk/wp-content/uploads/sites/2/2015/05/Press-Journal-Newspaper-Media-Pack_May-2015.pdf

219. David Hutchison, 'If Scotland votes no, the media may well get the blame' *The Conversation*, 20 June 2014 http://theconversation.com/if-scotland-votes-no-the-media-may-well-get-the-blame Accessed 07 May 2015

220. Asa Briggs and Peter Burke, *Social History of the Media: From Gutenberg to the Internet*, (Cambridge: Polity, 2005) p. 165

221. Kemp, p. 56

222. Ibid. p. 52

223. Reid, p. 58

224. Dominic Ponsford, 'Survey reveals importance of media in helping Scots make referendum decision', *Press Gazette*, https://www.pressgazette.co.uk/survey-reveals-importance-media-helping-scots-make-referendum-decision 16 October 2014

225. Ian Jack, 'The Scottish press is in decline – could it hold an independent Scotland to account?' *Guardian*, 2 May 2014

226. Douglas, p. 164

227. Linklater, p. 28

228. Alan Taylor, 'Then and Now: A View From the Fourth Estate,' *Scottish Review of Books*, Vol. 10 No. 3 2014 p. 4

229. Benedict Anderson, *Imagined Communities: Reflections on the Origin and Spread of Nationalism,* (London: Verso, 2006) p. 6

230. Craig Calhoun, 'Introduction' *Habermas and the public sphere,* (Cambridge, MA: MIT Press, 1992) p. 2

231. Ernest Renan, 'What is a Nation' *Nation and Narration,* ed. Homi K Bhabha, pp. 8-21 p. 11

232. Cowan, p. 20

6. Spaces of Autonomy

233. Manuel Castells, *Networks of Outrage and Hope,* (Cambridge: Polity, 2012) p. 2

234. 'George Square Trouble: The night our readers became reporters' *Sunday Herald*, 21 September 2014

235. Peter Geoghegan, 'After the Referendum' *London Review of Books*, Vol. 36 No. 19, 9 October 2014

236. Stuart Campbell, 'Enough is Enough' *Wings Over Scotland,* http://wingsoverscotland.com/enough-is-enough/ 20 September 2014 Accessed 01 June 2015

237. Neal Ascherson, *Stone Voices: the Search for Scotland*, (London: Granta, 2013) p. 108

238. Neal Ascherson 'After the Referendum' *London Review of Books*, Vol. 36 No. 19, 9 October 2014

239. Paul Mason, *Why It's Kicking Off Everywhere*, (London: Verso, 2013) p. 80

240. Angela Haggerty, 'The Scottish media's indyref story: The *Scotsman*, *Sunday Herald*, STV and Scotland's new media on how they shaped the debate' *The Drum*, http://www.thedrum.com/news/2014/09/18/scottish-medias-indyref-story-scotsman-sunday-herald-stv-and-scotlands-new-media-how 18 September 2014

241. Mike Small, 'Media wars' *Bella Caledonia* 6 October 2013

242. Robert Cookson, 'Yes campaign winning social media battle in Scotland, says Facebook', *Financial Times*, 16 September 2014

243. RecordView, 'Wings Over Scotland website fuels hatred and paranoia' *Daily Record*, 25 February 2015

244. http://wingsoverscotland.com/wp-content/uploads/2015/07/euro-pepoll.jpg

245. Mădălina Ciobanu, 'How The Ferret will 'nose up the trousers of power' *Journalism.co.uk* 29 May 2015 https://www.journalism.co.uk/news/how-the-ferret-will-nose-up-the-trousers-of-power-/s2/a565289/ Accessed 01 June 2015

246. Stuart Allan, *Citizen Witnessing*, (Cambridge: Polity, 2013) p. 9

247. Nick Davies, *Flat Earth News*, (London: Vintage, 2009) p. 395

248. Tamara Witschge, 'Street journalists versus 'ailing journalists'?' *Open Democracy* 27 March 2009 https://www.opendemocracy.net/article/street-journalists-as-an-answer-to-ailing-journalism Accessed 30 June 2015

249. Allan, p. 206

250. Axel Burns, 'Produsage: Towards a Broader Framework for User-Led Content Creation' *In Proceedings Creativity & Cognition* 6, 2007

251. William Davies, 'What have we lost in the shift from cigarettes to smartphones?' *OurKingdom* 12 March 2015https://www.opendemocracy.net/ourkingdom/william-davies/what-have-we-lost-in-shift-from-cigarettes-to-smartphones

252. Clay Shrikey, *Cognitive Surplus*, (London: Penguin, 2011) p. 161-162

253. Burns, p. 4

254. James Curran and Jean Seaton, *Power Without Responsibility: The Press and Broadcasting in Britain*, (London: Routeledge, 1997) p. 49

255. Raymond Williams, *Culture and Materialism*, (London, Verso, 2005) p. 211

256. Asa Briggs and Peter Burke, *Social History of the Media: From Gutenberg to the Internet*, (Cambridge: Polity, 2005) p. 213

257. Ibid, p. 213

258. Kemp p. 51

259. Ithiel de Sola Pool, *Technologies of Freedom*. (Cambridge, MA: Harvard University Press. 1983) p. 5

260. Joshua Meyrowitz, 'No Sense of Place' in *The Media Reader: Continuity and Transformation* ed. Hugh Mackay, Tim O'Sullivan (London: Sage, 1999) p. 106

7. Towards a Scottish Media

261. UNESCO, *Many Voices One World*, (Paris: UNESCO, 1980) p. 3

262. Christopher H Sterling, *Encyclopaedia of Journalism*, (London: Sage, 2009) p. 1012

263. Tony Ageh, 'The BBC, the licence fee and the digital public space' *openDemocracy*, 3 March 2015 https://www.opendemocracy.net/ourbeeb/tony-ageh/bbc-licence-fee-and-digital-public-space Accessed 30 March 2015

About the Author

Christopher Silver was raised in Shetland and now lives in Edinburgh. He has contributed words to *Prospect, openDemocracy, Bella Caledonia,* and *Scotland on Sunday* amongst others. In 2014 he edited a collection of art and writing, *Inspired by Independence* and produced a feature length documentary on grassroots politics in the referendum campaign, *Scotland Yet.* His first play *Forsaken* toured in April 2015. He is also the producer of *Two Minute Manifesto,* a monthly podcast and live show about politics, culture and ideas.

@silverscotland
christophersilver.co.uk